INFORMATION LITERACY

**Educating Children
For the 21st Century**

INFORMATION LITERACY

Educating Children For the 21st Century

by

PATRICIA SENN BREIVIK

and

J.A. SENN

SCHOLASTIC
LEADERSHIP
POLICY
RESEARCH ™

New York • Toronto • London • Auckland • Sydney

Copyright ©1994 by Scholastic Inc.

No part of this publication may be reproduced in whole or in part, or stored in a retrieval system, or transmitted in any form or by any means, electronic, mechanical, photocopying, recording, or otherwise, without permission of the publisher. For information regarding permission, write to Scholastic Inc., 555 Broadway, New York, NY 10012.

ISBN 0-590-49276-4

12 11 10 9 8 7 6 5 4 3 2 1   1 2 3 4 5/9

Printed in the U.S.A.

Library of Congress Cataloging-in-Publication Data

Breivik, Patricia Senn.
   Information literacy: educating children for the 21st century/
  by Patricia Senn Breivik and J. A. Senn.
   p.   cm.
   Includes bibliographical references (p.) and index.
   ISBN 0-590-49276-4
   1. Library orientation for school children—United States. 2. Research—Study and teaching (Elementary)—United States. 3. Information retrieval—Study and teaching (Elementary)-United States. 4. Active learning—United States.
   I. Senn, J. A. II. Title.
Z711.2.B747   1994
025 5'678—dc20
                                                                 93-34797
                                                                        CIP

Designed by Joan Gazdik Gillner

Dedication

This book is dedicated to the elementary school principals who, despite all odds, are responding creatively to the nationwide demand for schools to prepare young people for lifelong learning in today's Information Age. In trying to make their students' lives better, these dedicated principals are ultimately making a difference in the future of the United States. This book is, therefore, written as a tribute to them—as well as to the school library media specialists and teachers who work with them.

This book is also dedicated to our two favorite lifelong learners, Kenneth and Penni; and it could not have been completed without the patience and very hard work of Kris Kelly, Sylvia Spring, and Beth Walsh.

Patricia Senn Breivik

J. A. Senn

CONTENTS

Preface ix
Major Contributors x

1. SURVIVING IN AN INFORMATION AGE — 1

2. A COMMONSENSE APPROACH — 9
Information Literacy **10**
Resource-Based Learning **11**
Curriculum Integration **16**
Collaborative Planning **20**
Information Literacy Plans **23**
Resource-Based Learning Units **24**

3. SPECIFIC CONCERNS — 31
Mainstreaming **32**
Cultural Diversity **34**
Academically Disadvantaged **39**
Lifelong Readers **41**
Technology **45**
National Education Goals **51**

4. OVERCOMING BARRIERS — 55
Fixed Library Schedules **56**
Teacher Resistance **60**
Inadequate Resources **63**
Impatience **64**
Staff Development **65**

5. YOUR INVESTMENT — 71
Staffing **71**
Collections **75**
Equipment **78**
Automation and Resource Sharing **80**
Additional Funding **82**

6. CONNECTING WITH COMMUNITY RESOURCES —— 87
    Connecting with Community Members..............**88**
    Connecting with Public Libraries.....................**97**
    Connecting with Businesses.............................**103**
    Other Connections..**110**

7. ASSESSMENT OF RESOURCE-BASED LEARNING —— 115
    Independent Assessment..................................**116**
    School Assessments..**121**
    Need for Additional Assessment......................**127**

8. MOVING FORWARD —— 131
    Begin with Yourself..**132**
    Develop a Vision...**134**
    Introduce the Vision...**136**
    Build Support for the Vision.............................**138**
    Obtain the Vision..**141**
    Possess the Rewards of the Vision...................**146**

CLOSING THOUGHTS —— 148

SELECTED READING LIST —— 150

APPENDIXES
    A. ALA Presidential Committee on Information Literacy: Final Report..............**153**
    B. Washington State Information Skills Curriculum Scope and Sequence K–12..............**169**
    C. National Education Goals and the Four Strategy Tracks Identified in *America 2000: An Education Strategy*..............**178**
    D. National Forum on Information Literacy Membership List..............**179**
    E. Christina S. Doyle's 1992 Executive Summary as It Relates to National Education Goal III..............**180**
    F. Implementing the Colorado State Board of Education Goals through School Library Media Programs..............**182**
    G. Highlights from *The Impact of School Library Media Centers on Academic Achievement*..............**185**

PREFACE

At one time people were considered literate if they could write their names, but as society became more complex, the definition of *literacy* gradually evolved to encompass the abilities needed to function within the changing society. But what abilities are actually required in this modern society? Does modern literacy, for example, mean having the ability to read and memorize facts, or does it mean knowing where to find the facts and how to evaluate them? Indeed, in this new Information Age of online databases, interactive video disks, and so many other seemingly limitless sources of information, *literacy* must be redefined as *information literacy*—as the ability to acquire and evaluate whatever information is needed at any given moment.

The American Library Association's 1989 report on information literacy states that "to respond effectively to an ever-changing environment, people need more than just a knowledge base, they also need techniques for exploring it, connecting it to other knowledge bases, and making practical use of it. In other words, the landscape upon which we used to stand has been transformed, and we are being forced to establish a new foundation called *information literacy*."

Such a transformed landscape, of course, presents a particular challenge to educators everywhere to guarantee that all students are information-literate before they graduate so that they can live healthy, satisfying, and productive lives as adults. This book has been written to address that challenge in a very practical way. For example, after the first two chapters, which provide the necessary conceptual framework for discussion, the book gives real-life examples of the exciting things that are currently happening in schools scattered across the country, and it also tells you what you need to know to make your students information-literate—starting today!

It should also be noted that we have chosen to address elementary school principals in this book because they—more than anyone else in an elementary school—can open doors and make the changes necessary to produce information-literate students. However, this book is really an open conversation directed at all educational leaders, and, for that matter, at anyone who is concerned about educating today's youngsters for the 21st century.

The Authors

Major Contributors

This list of contributors is unusual in that those named below did not literally write any part of this book. What they did do, however, was sit with us, the authors, and share with us their personal experiences with resource-based learning—both their triumphs and their heartaches. As you read this book, you will see that there could not have been a book without them.

Ruth Bell, Director of Library Media Services
Blue Valley School District
15020 Metcalf, Overland Park, KS 66223

Terry Blevins, Volunteer Coordinator
Iowa City Community School District
509 South Dubuque, Iowa City, IA 52240

Thomas J. Cilek, Senior Vice President
Hills Bank and Trust Company
132 E. Washington Street, Iowa City, IA 52240

Sharon Coatney, Library Media Specialist
Oak Hill Elementary School
10200 W. 124th St., Overland Park, KS 66213

Susan Dangremond, Principal
Lakeview Elementary School
752 Lugers Road, Holland, MI 49423

Nancy L. Dobrot, Director of Library Services
Northside Independent School District
5900 Evers Road, San Antonio, TX 78238

Susan Geiger, Library Media Specialist
Clearspring Elementary School
9930 Moyer Road, Damascus, MD 20872

Janadene Harvey, Principal
Ernest Horn Elementary School
600 Koser Avenue, Iowa City, IA 52246

Lillian Krasner, Jeanne Bouga-Rose,
 Glenn Pribek
Resource Room Teachers at North Side School
110 East Williston Avenue, East Williston, NY 11596

Bernice Lamkin, Director
Regional Educational Media Center 7
13565 Port Sheldon Road, Holland, MI 49424

Marian Lattanzio, Head of Children's Services
Lucy Robbins Welles Library
95 Cedar Street, Newington, CT 06111

Dean F. Pacholl, Library Media Specialist
604 5th Avenue, SW
Austin, MN 55912

Fran Rhodes, Principal
R. B. Fernandez Elementary School
6845 Ridgebrook, San Antonio, TX 78250

Kim Carter (Sands), Information Specialist
Souhegan High School
412 Boston Post Road, Amherst, NH 03031

Diane Skorupski, Library Media Specialist
Liberty Elementary School
P.O. Box 11280, Tucson, AZ 85734

Alan Thormeyer, Principal
Clearspring Elementary School
9930 Moyer Road, Damascus, MD 20872

Ellen Tirone, Library Media Specialist and
 her colleagues at the Harold Martin School
Main Street, Hopkinton Village, Contoocook, NH 03229

Jean Donham van Deusen, Library Media
 Coordinator
Iowa City Community School District
509 South Dubuque Street, Iowa City, IA 52240

CHAPTER 1
SURVIVING IN AN INFORMATION AGE

> **"** Information—being able to process information and making personal meaning from information—is the number one thing businesses need from our students today—as well as in the future."
>
> KIM CARTER (SANDS), INFORMATION SPECIALIST,
> SOUHEGAN HIGH SCHOOL, AMHERST, NH

THINK OF THE INCREDIBLE RANGE OF INFORMATION that you and your family need over a short period of time, and then consider how those needs often splinter into a series of other needs.

- What car should I buy? Should I buy a new or used one? Which dealer should I do business with? Where should I get the financing?
- What are the alternatives to elderly parents living on their own? What care facilities are available? How can my parents' finances be protected?
- Which candidate will do the best job on the City Council? Which of them has the best approach to economic development? What has been their position on earlier community issues?
- How serious is the medical condition that the doctor says I have? Which of the treatments would be best? What are the possible side effects of the treatments? What kind of support groups exist? Should I get a second opinion?

- To which of the many requests for donations should I respond?
- Which of the community service clubs should I join?
- Which book should I buy?
- How much should I pay for an air conditioner?
- How do I find a good repairperson?
- Which movies are suitable for young children?
- Should I get an extended warranty on my new VCR?
- What is the best investment I can make with the $1,000 I just inherited?

Answering these and many other questions about daily life necessitates the finding, accessing, and using of different sources of information. Think also of the many other needs you have for incorporating information management skills into your professional life.

- What workshops or college courses might benefit me or my staff? How do I know which ones are worth the time and expense?
- What are some ways I could build helpful partnerships with the business community?
- Where can I find reliable computer software reviews?
- Where can I refer parents who need literacy training?

Although you may never have to—nor want to—prepare for a whole new career before you retire, it is estimated that most young people in school today will face four career changes during their lifetimes. Is your school preparing young people for such drastic changes? In fact, is your school preparing students to make wise decisions in all the complex situations that our society thrusts upon them?

Given the above realities, it should come as no surprise that almost all of the educational reform reports of the 1980s recommended preparing students for lifelong learning. There is, in fact, no way anyone any longer can achieve a reasonable quality of life without being a lifelong learner. However, those same reports scarcely acknowledged the unique challenges posed by today's rapidly changing data-rich Information Age. One exception was the 1989 *American Library Association Presidential Committee on Information Literacy: Final Report,* which states the following.

> No other change in American society has offered greater challenges than the emergence of the Information Age. Information is expanding at an unprecedented rate, and enormously rapid strides are being made in the technology for storing, organizing, and accessing the ever growing tidal wave of information. The combined effect of these factors is an increasingly fragmented information base—large components of which are only available to people with money and/or acceptable institutional affiliations.
>
> Yet in an information society all people should have the right to information that can enhance their lives. Out of the super-abundance of available information, people need to be able to obtain specific information to meet a wide range of personal and business needs. These needs are largely driven either by the desire for personal growth and advancement or by the rapidly changing social, political, and economic environments of American society. What is true today is often outdated tomorrow. A good job today may be obsolete next year. To promote economic independence and quality of existence, there is a lifelong need for being informed and up-to-date.
>
> How our country deals with the realities of the Information Age will have enormous impact on our democratic way of life and on our nation's ability to compete internationally. Within America's information society, there also exists the potential of addressing many long-standing social and economic inequities. To reap such benefits, people—as individuals and as a nation—must be information literate. To be information literate, a person must be able to recognize when information is needed and have the

ability to locate, evaluate, and use effectively the needed information. Producing such a citizenry will require that educators at both the school and college levels appreciate and integrate the concept of information literacy into their learning programs and that they play a leadership role in equipping individuals and institutions to take advantage of the opportunities inherent within the information society.

Ultimately, information literate people are those who have learned how to learn. They know how to learn because they know how knowledge is organized, how to find information, and how to use information in such a way that others can learn from them. They are people prepared for lifelong learning, because they can always find the information needed for any task or decision at hand. [p. 1] (See Appendix A on page 153 for the full report.)

Although there has not been a literal explosion—such as the following cartoon suggests—there is no doubt about the reality of the phenomenon of the information explosion.

Reprinted with special permission of King Features Syndicate

Some educators, however, have little appreciation of how the information explosion affects them and how they can best position themselves, their families, their special interest groups, and their schools to make the riches offered by this information society work for them—rather than against them.

To help increase your appreciation of the impact of the information explosion, picture the classic episode of "I Love Lucy," in which Lucy and Vivian are working on an assembly line in a candy factory. At first all goes well, and they cheerfully wrap each piece of chocolate as it moves by them on the conveyer belt. Soon, however, the belt begins to pick up speed. No matter what they do, Lucy and Vivian cannot slow down the rush of candies; and their coping skills are quickly exhausted despite their creative and increasingly desperate efforts to keep up with the overwhelming flood of candies.

While this scene has brought much laughter to television viewers, the situation loses its humor when you compare the candy to the overwhelming flood of information that daily bombards you. For example, place yourself in your capacity as an educator in Lucy's situation. How well do you manage the flow of information? How well do you keep up with all of the reports, journal articles, TV programs, and books that pour out year after year on the topic of education? What do you know about computer networks? Should you try to get your school hooked up to Internet or to some network that specializes in K–12? How many of the available networks could actually benefit your school? How can you find out? Finally, out of hundreds of thousands of pieces of information, how can you find those few items that really interest you and really could make a difference to the students in your school? Now, picture yourself as a worker not only on the assembly line of educational information but also on all of the other assembly lines producing all the other information important to your personal and civic responsibilities!

Computers have been both the major cause and greatest facilitator of this Information Age. In fact, computer technology has proven invaluable for the quick retrieval of short pieces of information and for the sharing of information among networked scholars and researchers. By and large, however, computer technology has not made information management easier; indeed, it has actually created many new problems. For example, people have a tendency to have more faith in information they see on a computer screen than in information they get from any other source. However, computer generated information should certainly be taken with a grain of salt because the data that are put into the computer can be incorrect and the software that manipulates the data can be flawed.

Most people, moreover, believe that computer databases are comprehensive when, in fact, only a very small portion of existing information exists in computer-readable formats. On the other hand, a growing number of people worry about the gap between the "have's" and the "have-not's" that is widening because of the costs involved in accessing information through new technologies.

In spite of the problems inherent in computers, they have created overwhelming changes in the workplace. In the December 1, 1992, issue of the *Wall Street Journal,* for example, the internationally respected consultant and professor of management Peter Drucker warns, "Executives have become computer-literate. The younger ones, especially, know more about the way the computer works than they know about the mechanics of the automobile or the telephone. But not many executives are information literate. They know how to get data. But most still have to learn how to use data."

Drucker goes on to emphasize, 'Few executives yet know how to ask: "What information do I need to do my job? When do I need it? In what form? And from whom should I be getting it?' Fewer still ask: 'What new tasks can I tackle now that I get all these data? Which old tasks should I abandon? Which tasks should I do differently?'" He concluded by stressing, "A 'database,' no matter how copious, is not information. It is information's ore. For raw material to become information, it must be organized for a task, directed toward specific performance, applied to a decision. Raw material cannot do that itself."

Beyond the raw material of online databases, there are, of course, an almost limitless number of other sources of information that you and the students in your school will need from time to time because of their content, timeliness, or type of presentation. There are, for example, the just-released annual report to stockholders, the latest survey results of a citizens' action group, and the newspaper article about health care by a well-respected doctor—to name just a few.

Perhaps the most common source of information today is television. In fact, throughout their lives, children will watch more hours of television than they will spend in school. Because toy manufacturers understand the strong influence of television on children, they spend millions of dollars a year to advertise their products, and increasing numbers of advertisers of adult products are targeting young children to build brand loyalty for future sales. While some parents and educational leaders bristle at the idea of Whittle Communications' offer to provide video equipment to schools that agree to show some programming that includes advertisements, these same people have been far slower to deal with the issue of how to get children to be savvy consumers of all televised information—including advertisements.

The end result of this bombardment of information is, as Richard Saul Wurman has aptly named it, *information anxiety*. Other writers have also cautioned that information technology leaves less time for reflection, and as a result, the problems it causes rarely find solutions because the flow of information continues to increase.

Kim Carter (Sands), an information specialist at the Souhegan High School in Amherst, New Hampshire, and the 1991 New Hampshire Teacher of the Year, summed up this bombardment of information in a recent interview when she stated, "In 1954, information doubled every 20 years; now it doubles every 30 to 36 months. By the year 2000, it will double every 12 or 18 months. Given these realities, what kind of graduates are going to be needed for the workplace?" Pausing for a moment, she continued, "Just look at society. The evidence is there. Information—being able to process information and making personal meaning from information—is the number one thing businesses need from our students today—as well as in the future." She concluded by saying, "No longer can anyone do without information skills."

Producing such information-literate students is what resource-based learning—and this book—are all about!

CHAPTER 2
A COMMONSENSE APPROACH

> "Ultimately, information literate people are those who have learned how to learn . . . because they can always find the information they need for any task or decision at hand."
>
> FROM THE AMERICAN LIBRARY ASSOCIATION
> PRESIDENTIAL COMMITTEE ON INFORMATION LITERACY: FINAL REPORT

IT IS SAFE TO ASSUME THAT ELEMENTARY SCHOOL PRINCIPALS did not enter into their profession for money because nobody decides to go into elementary education to become rich. Another sure thing is that elementary school principals are not sitting around wondering what to do with all their free time. Being a good elementary school principal has never been an easy job, and the demands on principals have significantly increased since the 1980s because of concerns for curriculum reform, site-based management, community involvement, and student outcomes assessment. Yet, despite the ever growing number of challenges confronting them daily, many principals still have been able to carve out enough time to become the instructional leaders of their schools.

This book contains excerpts from interviews with several of these principals from across the country as well as the school library media specialists and teachers who work with them. We, the authors of this book, are in some ways mere reporters of what we have seen and heard, and this book is our way of sharing with you the exciting stories and the good advice of these professionals who are harnessing the riches of the Information Age in order to create more active learning environments for their students. Their efforts are resulting not only in increased learning opportunities for all their students but also in the development of ardent lifelong readers and learners. Their approach to curriculum reform, as you shall see, also puts the fun back into learning for students and makes teaching a lot more rewarding.

INFORMATION LITERACY

Sooner or later schooling is over for everyone, and the teacher is no longer there to hand out textbooks or to say what is important to learn. As a result, students must become information detectives who can readily find the information they need in any situation and who can weigh the truthfulness of the evidence they find. Only if they are experienced information detectives upon graduation will they be prepared for lifelong learning, a necessary prerequisite for living well in the 21st century.

Although concerns for the impact of this information-overloaded world were absent from most of the reform reports of the 1980s, such an omission is not too surprising. After all, most of the people who wrote those reports had completed their own educations before the implications for education during the change from an industrial society to an information society were clear. Basically, their mind-set in evaluating educational practices and recommending improvements was as outdated as the one-room schoolhouse. Few, if any, were able to envision today's classrooms, which can encompass the whole world through available information and technologies. Moreover, most of the people who wrote those reports had had positive school experiences in far less complex times and who, therefore, thought largely in terms of the way they had been taught. To some extent they could all relate to the often-asked question: "Why can't we go back to the basics?"

It is clear, however, that education cannot go back to the basics. Even if it could, it would never be the same because today's elementary schools must operate in an ever-expanding and ever-changing environment. Today, for example, students must learn how to be information savvy. They must be able to find information on any topic and then be able to evaluate the quality of that information and its suitability for the task at hand. They also need to know how to organize and produce information products. In short, they need to be information literate.

Information literacy has been defined in the *American Library Association Presidential Committee on Information Literacy: Final Report* as the abilities to

- know when there is a need for information,
- identify information needed to address a given problem or issue,
- find needed information,
- evaluate the information,
- organize the information, and
- use the information effectively to address the problem or issue at hand. [p. 1]

The information-literate person, therefore, has mastered the abilities to locate, organize, evaluate, and communicate information. The information-literate person is thus empowered for effective decision making, for freedom of choice, and for participation in a democratic society.

RESOURCE-BASED LEARNING

To achieve information literacy, students must be given repeated opportunities to work with the same information resources that will bombard them throughout their lives. To help their students become information literate, teachers—supported by school library media specialists—must move away fron single-text teaching and focus on exposing students to real-world information resources and technologies.

Susan Dangremond, principal of the Lakeview Elementary School in Holland, Michigan, echoed this concern when she said, "I had heard the statistic that information was doubling every two-and-a-half years, and I realized immediately that teaching facts from a textbook just wasn't going to work any longer." She added, "I also realized that if students were taught library skills in isolation, they weren't going to mean anything. Children have to have something to hook this information on to; they have to be able to apply it if they are going to internalize the learning."

Principal Dangremond's expressed concern eventually led her to *resource-based learning*, which is defined in the 1977 *International Dictionary of Education* as "a learning mode wherein the pupil learns from his own interaction with a range of learning resources rather than from class expository." Janadene Harvey, principal at the Ernest Horn Elementary School in Iowa City, clarified the meaning of *resource-based learning* when she said, "In my mind, resource-based learning is very different than just providing a teacher with a hundred books, five videotapes, three filmstrips, and two audiotapes about some topic." She explained, "It truly is spending the time to look at the topic, deciding what are the major issues the teacher wants to cover in relationship to that topic, and finding the materials that will help the children meet those outcomes. I really believe that resource-based learning must involve an integration of the services of the media center and of the media specialist into daily classroom instruction."

At one and the same time, a resource-based learning approach to the curriculum is both so familiar as to be overlooked and so different as to require a paradigm shift. It is familiar because most teachers have always been involved in

resource-based learning to some extent—such as
- having students report on newspaper articles,
- having community or career experts make classroom presentations,
- taking students to museums and zoos, and
- sending students to the library to find information on particular topics.

All of these experiences expose students to the larger scope of information that exists beyond the classroom and beyond the walls of the school. While these activities have some value in and of themselves, as curriculum add-ons, they fail to achieve one of the major goals of resource-based learning, which is to infuse learning resources into the curriculum.

Resource-based learning is actually a commonsense approach to learning. If students are to continue learning throughout their lives, they must be able to access, evaluate, organize, and present information from all of the real-world sources of information that surround them—such as television, books, magazines, online databases, government agencies, experts, and, of course, libraries. However, such learning resources must become an integral part of the learning process instead of being add-ons to a hit-or-miss approach.

If resource-based learning is to become a reality, teachers can no longer herd students into their classrooms and keep them corralled there with their lectures and textbooks. Instead, they must become involved in a new kind of collaborative learning environment. Teachers, library media specialists, and others must work together to create an integrated approach to the curriculum, and for their part, students must begin to assume more responsibility for their own learning. When used to its fullest, resource-based learning will cause a major paradigm shift within most schools—as is illustrated by Figure 2.1—by redefining long-established educational roles and concepts.

Preparation for Lifelong Learning. Apparent from the interviews with principals was their sense of an overwhelming need to prepare students for a world very different from the one for which they had been educated. Each one of them, in fact, articulated why they believed that resource-based learning was the best way to prepare students for lifelong learning in a rapidly changing society. For example, Principal Dangremond, explaining how she and her staff moved toward resource-based learning over a period of time, said, "As a staff we spent two years studying and discussing learning styles. After we had gained a basic understanding of individual styles, it only made sense to us to integrate all of the areas of the curriculum in order to help children learn how to access, process, and communicate information." She concluded by saying, "We realized there was a need to develop independent learners, and for that to happen, we couldn't just pour facts into the students anymore. We had to give them tools—a process—by which they could become their own best teachers."

Fran Rhodes, principal of the R. B. Fernandez Elementary School in San Antonio, similarly stated her belief that resource-based learning produces better learners than a traditional teaching approach. She said, "Children as well as adults do not learn—really learn—in isolation, but an integrated library program makes it possible for students to identify needs and to acquire information resources as they work toward meeting those needs." She continued, "Therefore, as students go back and forth between the classroom and the

FIGURE 2.1

Paradigm Shifts

FROM ▷ ▷ ▷ ▷ ▷ ▷ ▷ TO

Information Is Power

What is...	What ought to be...
textbook as source	variety of media/sources
teacher as teller	teacher as guide/coach
facts are primary	questions are primary
information is packaged	information is discovered
assessment:	multivariable assessment:
seat work	synthesis
test scores	application
grades	students produce
	teachers critique
	demonstration
	test scores
	grades

Developed by the Grand Haven School District, Grand Haven, MI library, they get a sense of continuity. From what I now know about learning, how people learn, and what makes learning real, resource-based learning is the right way to go."

CURRICULUM INTEGRATION

Before going any further, it is time to whet your appetite for the excitement and fun of resource-based learning by describing a typical resource-based instructional unit. By reading about the unit now, you will also become aware of another theme that consistently appears in the interviews for this book. That theme is the need to integrate the various subject matters within the learning process, because students do not approach life—nor do they think—in neat, discrete disciplines. Moreover, their daily interactions outside of school are not packaged in self-contained disciplines. The long established word problems in math, for example, were an attempt to address students' need to use their knowledge in real-world settings, but the problems were usually so simplified and divorced from the realities of life that they held little meaning for children. How many people, for instance, will ever have a need to calculate where two trains heading toward each other at different rates of speed will meet?

Besides the value of matching students' thinking patterns and techniques for solving real problems, there is another important reason for integrating the curriculum. Because there are so many required subjects (in public schools the curriculum is often determined by state regulations), there simply are not enough hours in the day to separately teach each one. To the basics have been added topics related to drugs and alcohol, sex education, environmental concerns, and so on. Sharon Coatney, the library media specialist at the Oakhill Elementary School in Overland Park, Kansas, reported that this concern as a primary motivating factor in the planning efforts at her school. She said, "Our teachers need to integrate more because they cannot possibly teach everything they are required to cover. As a result, we are constantly working on more efficient ways to cover everything in time-saving ways—as well as to prepare students for lifelong learning."

The following example of an integrated resource-based instructional unit was developed by four teachers at the Lawrence Seventh Grade Center of Springfield (Illinois) School District #186. Even before the reform reports of the 1980s, these teachers were committed to integrating the curriculum, organizing the classroom for collaborative learning, and getting students to take more responsibility for their own learning. Planning as a team, they developed an archeology unit that integrated all the students' major subject areas.

At the beginning, the students were grouped into small teams. Each team was given a large box, sand, and a book for keeping a log of their research and planning. Then the teams were turned loose in the library media center to do research on a very early period of history. (Most of the teams studied prehistoric times.) They were to find out everything they could about such topics as how people lived, what they wore, what they ate, how they were sheltered, and what work they did.

Once their research was complete, the teams found or constructed "tokens of life" of their period. They placed these in sand near the bottom of their boxes to serve as archeological artifacts. The teams then recorded in their logs information on the lifestyle of the period and how the buried artifacts reflected that lifestyle. Afterwards, each team went on to research how people lived at several later periods of time. Near the end of the unit, the teams exchanged boxes, and the students became teams of archaeologists who sought to reconstruct and document the civilizations represented in the artifacts they "discovered" in another team's box. The project concluded with an evaluation in which the students matched their recorded archeological findings with the lifestyles previously recorded in the logs of the students who had created the "digs."

It is not difficult to imagine how all subject areas could be blended into such a unit. Historical research, for example, provides ample information for math studies centered around the currencies used by the various civilizations, and for science, the students could study the environmental issues of the various eras. Not only do the students learn the subject matter of the various disciplines, but they also gain experience in research, critical thinking, and working collaboratively—skills they will be able to carry over to the rest of their lives. And, of course, it is easy to imagine how much fun the students could have learning math, science, language arts, and social studies in this way.

Collaborative Learning. Collaborative learning is another hallmark of successful resource-based learning programs. As researchers have documented, learning is by nature a social activity; moreover, students gain lifetime benefits by learning to work with groups of students with diverse abilities and knowledge.

Most often collaborative learning takes place within a class—such as the archeology unit just described—or among classes at a particular grade level, but sometimes it even transcends grade levels. For example, Nancy L. Dobrot, director of media services at the Northside Independent School District in San Antonio, told a story about a collaborative learning project that involved both second and fourth graders. The story began when the fourth-grade teacher, realizing that the second grade teacher also wanted to do a unit on dinosaurs, suggested that their classes work together. Dobrot explained what happened next.

> Eventually the fourth graders taught the second graders the library skills they needed to help them do their research on dinosaurs. They read stories to the second graders, and they actually did all of the other things the librarian and the teachers would have done. Then each day after the second graders had gone back

to their classroom, the school library media specialist sat down with the fourth graders and asked, "Did you have any problems or questions you couldn't answer?" For the next 15 to 20 minutes—at that very point when everything was fresh in their minds—she addressed each issue they brought up. As a result, the fourth graders became stronger in their own skills each day.

(Chapter 6 describes two other collaborative projects that involve community members in addition to the school's media specialist, teachers, and students.)

Although the concepts of integrated and collaborative learning have been reoccurring themes in the curriculum reform movements of recent years, resource-based learning offers the only effective glue for holding such efforts together and for firmly connecting them with today's information-rich world. Principal Rhodes, commenting on the importance of this enriched approach to learning through integration and collaboration, said, "The planning and working together by the faculty and the librarian—as a team and as a community of learners—make it possible for the children's efforts to result in products that encompass everything the students have learned." Figure 2.2 on page 20 graphically depicts the overall skills outcomes that are obtained through such integration and collaboration.

COLLABORATIVE PLANNING

Learning opportunities—such as those previously described—can only result from collaborative planning. Although resource-based learning is a commonsense approach to education, it does not *just happen*. It requires collaboration at least between a single teacher and the library media specialist, but often it involves many more participants. Although collaborative curriculum planning frequently starts with one teacher and the library media specialist, it quickly grows as acceptance and enthusiasm build among those participating. As

FIGURE 2.2

INTEGRATIVE ROLE OF LIBRARY MEDIA CENTERS
Program Outcomes, Critical Learnings, and Essential Skills for School Library Media Programs

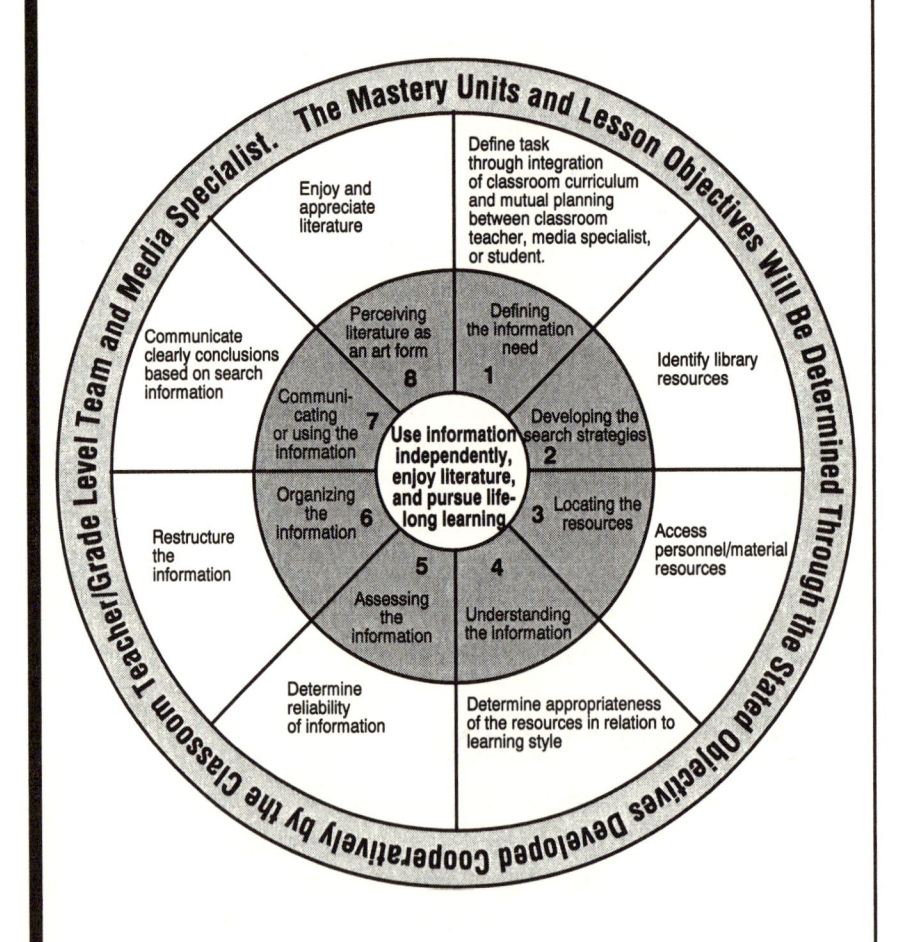

The Mastery Units and Lesson Objectives Will Be Determined Through the Stated Objectives Developed Cooperatively by the Classroom Teacher/Grade Level Team and Media Specialist.

Use information independently, enjoy literature, and pursue life-long learning

1. Defining the information need
   - Define task through integration of classroom curriculum and mutual planning between classroom teacher, media specialist, or student.
2. Developing the search strategies
   - Identify library resources
3. Locating the resources
   - Access personnel/material resources
4. Understanding the information
   - Determine appropriateness of the resources in relation to learning style
5. Assessing the information
   - Determine reliability of information
6. Organizing the information
   - Restructure the information
7. Communicating or using the information
   - Communicate clearly conclusions based on search information
8. Perceiving literature as an art form
   - Enjoy and appreciate literature

Developed by the Sunnyside Unified School, Tucson, AZ

20

a result, others become eager to try it at least once. Often this willingness to try then spreads to other teachers, and other classes. Sometimes even the entire school will get involved. Not infrequently the principal, as the instructional leader of the school, will also participate in at least the initial brainstorming sessions. *(For more information about the importance of collaborating and partnering, see Chapter 6.)*

There was also general agreement among those interviewed that one of the keys to successful collaborative planning is to begin with the curriculum requirements of each grade level and then think through what students can and should learn for themselves. Director Dobrot, for example, says that during collaborative planning sessions she always asks teachers, "What do you absolutely have to teach for your students to understand this unit?" Then she immediately follows that question with another one: "What can your students discover on their own?"

Another often heard comment was about the need to focus on the desired learning outcomes, including applied outcomes (products) that have immediate value for students. Such direction helps everyone, including parents, understand what to expect from students at particular points in their learning. Moreover, the immediate application of information skills and the satisfaction from the products that are created from the unit can be built upon continually until mastery occurs.

Susan Geiger, the library media specialist at the Clearspring Elementary School in Damascus, Maryland, emphasized this point when she said, "People don't want to learn how to do something if they don't see any reason for learning how to do it. For example, if I were building a treehouse and you offered to teach me how to use a power saw, I would be much more inclined to want to learn how to use it than if I were sitting down reading a book and you came up to me and asked, "How would you like to learn how to use a power saw?"

Information Specialist Carter (Sands) also explained this process clearly by means of the following example.

I think the key to all teaching—especially resource-based learning—is to set a goal. What is the goal of a particular unit, for example? What is the purpose for the students right now—not a year from now? You have to make sure you pull that thread through all of the planning and evaluation.

The goal, then, for a second grade weather unit was for the students to know enough about weather to be able to dress appropriately and to plan appropriate activities for themselves. As a result, the final evaluation for those kids was a picture from a children's literature book that illustrated a weather scene. Then we gave them a picture of a thermometer, an anemometer, and a barometer and asked them to write a weather report that said how to dress and what activities they could do. This goal was the catalyst that pulled together why they needed to have some understanding of such things as how the water cycle, cloud types, and wind speeds affect temperature. The end result was that the information the kids had gathered was immediate for them. If there is an immediate application, students will retain the information and eventually even be able to transfer it.

In summary, after the goals are chosen at collaborative planning sessions and the nature of the end products of those goals is decided, the next step is to determine what resources and services are available to facilitate learning. Then the real fun of learning begins as the students do their research and generate their products. When the products are completed, other students, school personnel, and parents are invited in to celebrate the students' learning outcomes, which may range from films to travel brochures or from online databases to bound books that are cataloged into the library media collection.

Finally, at schools committed to building on their successes, each unit ends with self-evaluation by those who planned it. During the evaluation process, the teachers and the media specialist add up the pluses and the minuses and decide what resources can ensure richer outcomes in the future. *(For more information about the evaluation of resource-based learning, see Chapter 7.)*

INFORMATION LITERACY PLANS

Many teachers and library media specialists have been evolving toward a resource-based learning approach over recent years—without knowing what to call it. This approach has come naturally to them as they have sought ways to individualize the learning process and to make learning more relevant to their students' out-of-school lives. Information Specialist Carter (Sands) summarized her own experiences by saying, "I think that there were many of us out there who were doing human-resource-based learning or just teaching with resources and learning, developing, and evolving toward resource-based learning because it felt right." She paused for a moment and then explained, "What I found was that initially it was something I got to do occasionally; it might be the icing on the cake to do a unit that way. However, once I had a name and structure for it, it became the focus of my efforts."

Once resource-based learning takes hold somewhere, a well-thought-out developmental plan usually follows to guide the systematic mastery of information management skills. Frequently these plans are available at the state level and are integrated with other state generated curriculum guides. *(For a good example of a state guideline, see the K–12 scope and sequence framework for the "Washington State's Information Skills Curriculum" in Appendix B on page 169.)* Local schools personalize such guidelines by considering the dynamics of their particular student populations and programs. Of course, where state plans or guidelines are not available, individual schools or districts must develop their own.

The basis for such plans has been documented by a number of people—such as Michael B. Eisenberg, Carol Ann and Ken Haycock, and Barbara K. Stripling. Each provides a similar framework for the planning efforts at the various grade levels. Normally, with an agreed upon template and starting at the kindergarten level, school personnel first determine a list of skills to be accomplished at each grade level. Then library media specialists work with teachers at each grade level to determine how best to accomplish those learning objectives within the teacher's subject-based lesson plans. Their collaborative work continues until a progressive information-management curriculum plan is established and understood by all of the teachers. Such planning, of course, takes time, but with administrative support, the process can move along quite quickly.

Besides planning, there are many other administrative and operational duties necessary to undergird the running of a successful resource-based learning program. *Information Power: Guidelines for School Library Media Programs,* which was prepared by the American Association of School Librarians and the Association for Educational Communications and Technologies, provides a series of helpful guidelines on issues such as personnel, facilities, equipment, and budgets. Most school library media specialists probably will have a well worn copy of this valuable resource close at hand. *(For more information about* Information Power, *see the Selected Reading List on page 150.)*

RESOURCE-BASED LEARNING UNITS

Since the proof is in the pudding, this chapter concludes with a sampling of resource-based learning units that have resulted from the type of planning efforts just described. However, a school that is just beginning a resource-based approach to learning may have to ease into such units. For example, often a media specialist will first use a commercially available multimedia package to model how integrated units actually work. Jean Donham van Deusen, the library media coordinator in the Iowa City Community School District, reported that "The Voyage of the Mimi" is a perfect piece to start with because "sometimes teachers need something like this program to show them how integration can work. Then they will be able to develop their own units."

"The Voyage of the Mimi," which won the *Classroom Computer Learning* "Ten Best Software Programs of the Year" award in 1986, is a multimedia package that combines video, computer software, and print materials and integrates concepts in math, science, social studies, and language arts. Among other things, it requires students to read maps, learn methods of navigation, create their own ecosystem, and work out simple computer programs. After introducing the software to the teachers at the Horace Mann School in Iowa City and implementing the program for the first time, Victoria Walton, the library media specialist, helped the teachers develop their own literature component to the program. From there they went on to create their own integrated units.

All of the following integrated resource-based instructional units have been collaboratively designed by teachers and school library media specialists—sometimes with the help of others such as art and music specialists and public librarians. In each unit, however, the learning resources were carefully integrated into the learning experience, and each learning experience resulted in tangible products that were usually shared with other students and/or parent or community groups.

Since the models are recorded here largely as they were provided to us, the amount of detail varies somewhat. Nevertheless, these examples should give you an idea of the extraordinarily wide range of subjects that integrated resource-based learning projects can encompass and the extraordinarily young age at which a child can start becoming information-literate. Most of these examples should also give you a few insights into what it would mean to your students to have the fun put back into learning—to replace the futility and senselessness they often feel with the status quo.

Kindergarten: Seasons. After the teacher covers a unit on the seasons, the students divide into four groups—one group per season. Each student then draws a picture of an activity that occurs during that season and dictates a sentence or two that describes the activity. After the teacher arranges the pictures in order of their occurrence during the season, the students go to the library media center and transfer their pictures to transparency film, using permanent ink overhead pens. Then they record their descriptions on audiotapes. At a gathering of parents and students, the kindergartners present their transparency show. Afterwards, they are allowed to take their transparencies home.

Kindergarten and First Grade: Researching. When the students go to the library media center to color leaves in the fall, the library media specialist asks them where they can find out what colors they should use for the leaves. Then she or he shows them how they can find out about leaves in magazines and books. As they research the different colors of leaves, they learn, for example, that they should not color their leaves blue because there are no blue leaves in the books or magazines. Afterwards, when a question comes up in the classroom that the students cannot answer, the teacher tells one or more students to put on a researcher's badge and go to the library media center to find the answer. Activities like this begin to teach students the value of research.

Grade 1: Symbols of the United States. During a unit about the United States, first graders go to the library media center where they read books about such U.S. symbols as the flag, the Pledge of Allegiance, and the national anthem. Then after researching the 27 flags in U.S. history, the students choose various ones and make facsimiles of them. Using software called "Timeliner," the children then make a timeline that displays each of the flags. As a part of the culminating activity, the children hang the timeline in the hallway and, as flag experts, they talk about the history of the different flags.

Grade 2: Native Americans. This three-and-a-half week unit brings together all disciplines covered in the second grade. For example, the students become familiar with myths and legends and write their own for language arts; they study various tribes and compare cultures for social studies; for science they study rocks, plants, and the seasons and how they impacted on Indian life; they investigate natural medicines for health, make masks for fine arts, and measure tools and study money systems for math—to name just some of the activities that the unit includes. In addition, various research skills—such as locating information and using a table of contents and index—are incorporated into the various content areas. At the conclusion of the unit, all of the products from the students' various efforts are displayed in the library media center and throughout the school.

Grade 3: Communities. To study their local communities, the third graders go to the library media center where they learn how to use a city map and the local telephone book to locate places of interest in the city. After noting on a local map what they want to find out, they go back to their classrooms and write to various places of interest to get information. Then, after students are shown how to use a camera, they are assigned a place of interest and are given a camera to take home. The parents are then responsible for taking their children to the particular place of interest so that they can take a picture of it. Once the pictures are developed, the students use the information they received from the place of interest to write captions to accompany their pictures. In the hallway, the pictures/captions are displayed around a large map of the city—with a piece of string going from each picture/caption to the place of interest on the map.

Grade 4: Poetry. Working with the teacher and the library media specialist, the fourth graders read poems from a variety of poetry books, keeping track of them in a log. Each student then selects one poem to share with the rest of the class by preparing a storyboard, a series of pictures and words in logical order, of the poem. After going though many stages, the storyboard is finally drawn on a blank filmstrip. Then the class members share their finished products with their "Poetry Partners." Evaluating this unit, one fourth grader said, "I thought poetry might be boring, but now I know it isn't."

Grade 5: Tall Tales. After the library media specialist introduces American tall tales and explains their characteristics to the fifth graders, each student reads several tall tales over a period of time. Eventually the students choose a favorite tall tale character or invent their own. Then they each write an original tall tale. With their stories in hand, they go to the library media center, where they learn how to produce a write-on filmstrip. Using a storyboard, the students first plan their pictures and then write narrations to accompany them. They are limited to 13 frames: title frame, credit frame, ten narrated pictures, and an end frame. After drawing their pictures on the storyboard, the students transfer their pictures to the filmstrip and record the narrations on 3 x 5 index cards or on audiotapes. The students then present their completed filmstrips to other students and their parents.

Grade 5: National Parks. First the fifth graders choose the two national parks that most interest them. Then they research each one to find out what its attractions are and why it is a national park. After locating both national parks on a map, they plan a trip between them. After doing research, the students write a two- or three-paragraph report, create a map, and produce a travel brochure that encourages other students to visit the parks they have chosen. During this unit, the fifth graders learn information skills such as using indexes and subheads and thinking skills such as recording and organizing. At the same time, they cover content areas such as science, math, and art.

Grade Six: The *Titanic*. To begin this unit, the teacher and the library media specialist present the question: "What would have made the outcome of the *Titanic* disaster different?" As the students work on finding the answer to this question, they cover material from many different subject areas. In math, for example, the sixth graders figure out such problems as the number of lifeboats available to the passengers and the distance between the *Titanic* and the rescue ship. For science, they study glaciers and displacement. For social studies, they look at social issues of the times that dictated class status and determined who got to abandon the ship first. Before writing an expository essay for language arts, the students take notes from videos as well as from books and other print resources. In class, they take all their acquired information and write an essay that answers the original question: "What would have made the outcome of the *Titanic* disaster different?"

Grade Six: Endangered Species. To challenge sixth graders to work with real-world problems, a five-week unit that meets the state environmental education requirement was designed around the topic of endangered species. The unit integrates language arts, environmental education, computing, art, and information literacy skills.

After the class acquires some general background information from various sources such as filmstrips, videos, and National Wildlife publications, small teams of students research specific animals. Their findings eventually result in the following:
- written reports with bibliographies,
- creative presentations (e.g., puppet show, magazine, TV show, "becoming" the animal),
- illustrations with captions, and
- editorials.

Multigrade Levels: Inventions. Each of several small groups of students is given a set of reference materials and a list of questions about a "fun" invention. Care is taken that each group has a strong reader and that each group's recorder fills in the answers to questions as they are found. To find the answers to the questions, the students use a variety of reference materials—such as *Children's Magazine Guide*, magazines, and encyclopedias.

Next, in their classrooms the group members share what they have learned and think about what is involved in inventing something. Then they are set free to use any resources they want to get ideas for an invention of their own. Once the students produce their inventions, an invention convention is set up in the library media center. There each child is videotaped talking about his or her invention. Parents, of course, are invited to come to see the inventions.

Several books provide other examples of resource-based learning units. Two of these, one by Michael Eisenberg and Robert Berkowitz and the other by Dean Pacholl, appear on the Selected Reading List on page 150. Both of these books also provide information on the organization and implementation of integrated instructional units.

CHAPTER 3
SPECIFIC CONCERNS

> " It's not so much a matter of dramatically turning away from an old teaching approach as it is of increasingly incorporating a resource-based approach to learning over a period of time."
>
> JANADENE HARVEY, PRINCIPAL OF THE ERNEST HORM ELEMENTARY SCHOOL IN IOWA CITY, IA

ALONG WITH THE FUNDAMENTAL CONCERNS FOR the quality of the teaching/learning process, there are some other more specific concerns with which educational leaders must often struggle. This chapter touches upon a few of them to show—in a representative way—how a resource-based approach to learning can be helpful in addressing the many problems confronting education today. Following is a list of the specific concerns that will be addressed in this chapter.

- The need to structure a learning environment that can accommodate students with diverse abilities and needs.
- The need to promote an appreciation for people of diverse backgrounds.
- The need to help academically disadvantaged students "catch up."
- The need to instill in children a desire to read and to foster good reading abilities.

- The need to effectively integrate technology into the curriculum.
- The need to respond to the challenge of the National Education Goals.

MAINSTREAMING

When people talk about "the good old days" in education and express a desire to return to them, they largely remember a homogeneous world. In those days, children with significant handicaps were not seen in regular classrooms, and IQ tests were used as the primary basis for separating the slower learners from the brighter ones. Under these circumstances, one textbook, one workbook, and largely one lesson plan seemed to meet, at least, reasonably well the educational needs of any one classroom of students.

"The good old days," of course, no longer exist. Today classrooms contain students with widely diverse learning abilities and learning styles. As a result, no one textbook, one workbook, or even one lesson plan can adequately meet the needs of all of these students, because some of the material is too hard for some and too easy for others, and some of it is downright boring to everyone. However, if teachers receive the support they need, they can move their students out into the larger world of the school library media center and, indeed, the community beyond the school. There it will be possible for students to find information on diverse topics that is written at their reading levels and/or is packaged in a manner best suited to their own learning styles. Schools then would no longer be in the business of hammering students into predetermined "holes."

In addition, a resource-based approach allows students the option of learning from more than one medium. Of course, improving reading levels and creating a desire to read should always be the priorities of every educator, but the truth is that reading simply is not the best way for all children to learn all subjects. Text alone or text with only minimal pictures does not reflect the normal life experiences of most children today who spend far more time watching television than reading. Children studying the Civil War, therefore, could benefit from viewing Ken Burns's excellent 1990 PBS documentary *The Civil War,* from seeing *Gone with the Wind,* and from studying a wealth of related print sources of information about this era. Depending on where they live, students would also greatly profit from observing or even participating in a reenactment of a Civil War battle and/or from touring actual battle sites. Such a variety in learning resources would naturally accommodate differing learning styles.

Moreover, some children learn best in groups. A few students, of course, can quickly grasp new ideas on their own, but many others benefit from the help of peers. For years educators have talked about individualizing the learning process to accommodate different learning styles, and for some time now testing has been able to determine preferred learning styles. Only when you add in resource-based learning, however, is there any real practical means—within reasonable budget limitations—of providing the rich variety in learning resources necessary to achieve an individualized approach to learning.

Resource-based learning has an additional benefit for students who lack home or peer encouragement for learning: immediate application. Most children, for example, can more easily relate their everyday worlds to newspapers, television news, government publications, and online databases, rather than to books exclusively. This multimedia approach even offers possibilities for parental involvement that more traditional school materials do not. There are, for instance, situations in which economically disadvantaged children, who have learned math through the Newspapers in Education program, have taught their parents how to save money by comparing prices advertised by various grocery stores. *(For more information about the Newspaper in Education program, see Chapter 6.)*

In summary, resource-based learning is a commonsense approach to addressing the wide range of student abilities and interests present in any typical classroom because it allows students—with the guidance of their teachers—to find and learn from materials that are at their comprehension levels and in formats and combination of formats that match their preferred learning styles. Resource-based learning also offers students increased motivation to learn because the materials are relevant to their out-of-school lives.

Clearspring Elementary School in Damascus, Maryland, is an outstanding example of how resource-based learning can effectively address the diverse needs of students. This school has integrated into the regular student body 45 multiply handicapped students who had previously studied at special schools. Alan Thormeyer, the principal of this school and the recipient of the *Washington Post's* Educational Leadership Award for 1990–1991, said, "These kids, who have been integrated as much as possible, are making it in a regular setting. They're doing it, and they're doing it well."

CULTURAL DIVERSITY

Of the many challenges facing education at all levels today, none is more emotionally charged than that of diversity. The old concept of the United States as a melting pot is giving way to the image of this country as a patchwork quilt that is beautiful in its range of colors and patterns. To be functionable, however, this quilt must have a backing of common beliefs that acknowledges the value of every individual and the importance of community. A balance between these beliefs is not easily achieved, but it is essential to the future well-being of this country and all of its citizens.

Some programs addressing this need to acknowledge diversity are clearly doomed to failure. For instance, requiring textbooks to include at least "one representative of each culture" before they are eligible for statewide adoption is certainly ill conceived. Asian and Hispanic people, for example, do not see themselves as generically Asian or Hispanic, but as very diverse population groups. Also, the attempt to acknowledge diversity often results in a generic blandness that fails to elicit any appreciation for people who are perceived as significantly different.

Bibliotherapy. For years educators have used an approach known as *bibliotherapy* to help children understand their own problems by enabling them to vicariously live through another's experiences. Hans Christian Andersen's story "The Ugly Duckling" is a good example of bibliotherapy because this story encourages young children who have not yet found their unique place among their peers to identify with the ugly duckling and find assurance that they, too, will live happier ever after. This same approach can be equally effective in promoting an appreciation of diverse cultures. Integrating such experiences into the curriculum through collaborative planning by teachers and library media specialists can further increase the benefits of vicariously experiencing someone else's life.

The following example clearly illustrates the value of engaging students' emotions as well as their intellects when the intent is to have them understand and appreciate others' pain and suffering. The following story was related by Gloria Rolton, who was a teacher for many years before becoming a teacher-librarian at the Blair Primary School in South Australia.

In 1986, as a Year 6 teacher, I began a social studies unit on Australian migration. Early in the discussion, one boy announced, "They are all wogs! We should send them back. Rambo has the right idea!" I could see my carefully planned program was doomed. In an effort to effect change, I began reading aloud Ian Strachan's *Journey of 1000 Miles*. This novel tells of the problems faced by a Vietnamese family when they left their home: the hardships they encountered on a small, overcrowded fishing boat; and the horrors from storms and pirates they had to endure. During the time we shared this book, the students were given the opportunity to "stand in someone else's shoes and see the world through their eyes."

The effect on the class was dramatic. There was an empathy and understanding that I could not have achieved through the discussion groups I had originally planned. At the culmination of the unit, I asked the class to prepare some creative writing from the point of view of a migrant. The boy who had previously made the Rambo comment wrote a paragraph that revealed a total reversal of attitude. *(See Figure 3.1 at the top of the next page.)*

This same general approach could be expanded by allowing students to read and/or view films or videos about young people from a number of different backgrounds. Subsequent sharing of first-person stories would also expose students to a variety of perspectives within a single class. The sharing of what has been learned, of course, does not always have to be in writing; it could just as effectively be expressed through a play or a bulletin board display.

Indeed, by drawing upon the richness of today's information resources and technologies, resource-based learning can address the challenge of cultural diversity with an almost limitless source of materials that can expose children to people of different races, colors, creeds, ages, and genders. Moreover,

FIGURE 3.1

> The day we left from Vetnam on a old fishing Boat stuck in my head because from that day on I felt like I was in a living death I left my friend and pets and most of all my loving parents I am in Sydny at a foster parents house My forster parents are tall be but nothing like my real parents in Vetnam. I feel ~~do~~ dumb and everybody treats me like a deviate from outa space exept my foster parents All the kids at our rotten school laugh, stare and pick on me. None of the people at oure school can say my name p~~ro~~ply [properly] so they either say "hey ya wag" or "Hey Kid." its ~~terribly~~ terrible. I'm always wondering if my parents are still alive ~~and~~ movies like "Rambo" and "First Blood" ~~be~~ don't help

through programs like the Western Technology Dream project, which is described later in this chapter, children can get to know and understand others who are culturally different by directly communicating with them.

Global Awareness. Closely related to the concern for promoting appreciation for diversity is the concern for increasing global awareness among students. As improved telecommunication and transportation systems seemingly shrink this world and as the economic and social conditions of other countries increasingly affect the United States, students need to be aware of the people and the cultures of those countries and to understand the connections to their own lives.

To illustrate how resource-based learning can add concreteness to a traditional geography lesson, Director Dobrot shared the experience of a fifth-grade class that was studying Africa. Originally the unit on Africa, which was contained in a thick workbook, had covered basic geography and a study of the African people. In addition, the fifth-grade teacher had pointed out the African countries on a wall map. She had also used ditto sheets, on which the children had written the answers to questions from her lectures.

Then one day when Dobrot was presenting a workshop on resource-based learning, the principal of that school challenged her to tell the teachers how she would reform the African unit to make it more meaningful. Dobrot began by asking the fifth-grade teachers two questions: What do you absolutely have to teach for your students to understand this unit? What can they discover on their own? In the ensuing discussion, the teachers realized that the students could discover almost all the information in their textbook by themselves.

Based on that conclusion, Dobrot suggested taking the students to the library media center, where they would learn to use the atlas and various other sources to research information about the African countries. Then she showed the teachers how they could incorporate math skills with the study of the atlas by asking students to determine longitudes and latitudes and how when covering dictionary skills they could encourage the students to develop a vocabulary with which to talk about the African cultures. She even pointed out that there were some very basic African/Swahili books in the library that the children could read.

Dobrot also showed the teachers how they could turn the material on the ditto sheets into questions that the students could address through research and various writing activities. Then she explained how the students could eventually make their information come alive by taking on the character of an African person and writing about that person's life. She concluded by telling the teachers, "Some could even make a connection to American history by researching those countries from which slaves had been brought over to America."

ACADEMICALLY DISADVANTAGED

Given children's significant differences in learning abilities and their varying degrees of motivation within a single classroom, one constant challenge for teachers is to simultaneously keep gifted children challenged, to build up the skills of academically disadvantaged children, and to keep the energies of the rest of the class engaged. It is a Herculean task at best; at worst the gaps in the knowledge and ability levels of children grow and get exacerbated at each succeeding grade level.

Through resource-based learning, however, teachers can contribute more effectively to the academic success of all their students. Principal Rhodes, for example, asserted that as a result of resource-based learning "all children in our school can learn. We put no limits on their learning; but in traditional and in ability-group approaches, there is a mind-set that certain children can learn 'this' with difficulty, and others can't possibly do it. That is no longer true for us."

Based on her experiences, Information Specialist Carter (Sands) stated, "One of the biggest payoffs of resource-based learning is the fact that as 'low level' [special ed] kids become comfortable with information sources, they begin to exhibit confidence; and once they start to feel confident about their work, they are also more willing to engage in learning." Continuing with enthusiasm, she said, "All of a sudden, they aren't failing; indeed, they not only are succeeding, but they are also succeeding with the rest of the class—instead of at a different pace or under different circumstances."

According to many of those interviewed, another major advantage of resource-based learning in closing the gap between the "have's" and "have-not's" is that it provides teachers with ongoing opportunities for special attention where needed. For example, in the case of the fourth graders who worked with the second graders on the dinosaur unit, which was described in Chapter 2, there was a special payoff for a few fourth graders who were behind in some of their math skills. Once their teacher had seen how well her students were working with the younger children—under the guidance of the second-grade teacher and the library media specialist—she was able to take them to another table in the library and work with them on their math skills.

In the example above, three different sets of learning needs were being simultaneously addressed, and it was even reported that "everyone had a good time with it!" In fact, at the R. B. Fernandez School in San Antonio, there have since been many more ungraded and cross-age cooperative learning projects, and peer tutoring is increasingly becoming a favorite teaching and learning tool. Information Specialist Carter (Sands) also reported that at her school in New Hampshire, "Resource-based learning took away the stigma that less academically prepared students often have because all groups of children are getting special attention throughout a unit at one time or another."

Director Dobrot echoed the importance of this kind of special attention, particularly during the first few grades when there are still a few students in the class who cannot read. Under a traditional approach, these students would not be able to participate in projects requiring reading skills. To illustrate her point, Dobrot described a unit on biographies that one class had done in the library media center.

> As the librarian was talking to three special needs students, she asked, "Where do we go to find information on this person?" One little boy who could not read answered, "The biographical dictionary!" Now there was a kid who couldn't read but who knew what book to go to! Because he also knew where the book was, the librarian read it to him and the other students. With her help, those kids were able to do the whole unit just as well as anyone else because she had time to spend with them since their teacher was there and the other kids were working on various tasks. Those who needed help, got it. Those who could work on their own were busily engaged. That's what learning in libraries is all about.

That is just one vivid example of how resource-based learning can help close the gap between students' abilities—rather than letting the gap widen year after year.

LIFELONG READERS

Certainly there is no educational shortcoming that is more devastating to a person's life than not being able to read. Only recently have Americans begun to acknowledge not only the number of adults who are functionally illiterate (many of whom are school graduates) but also the effects of illiteracy on the economy. Besides these illiterates, however, are the myriad individuals who can read but who seldom do so. According to the U.S. Department of Education, 44 percent of adults in the United States do not read even one book a year. Of course, other print media also are not read. For example, between 1967 and 1992, the percentage of adults who read a newspaper every day dropped from 73 percent to just below 50 percent. Jack W. Humphrey, project manager of the Middle Grades Reading Network at the University of Evansville in Evansville, IN, states in a March 1992 article in *Phi Delta Kappan* magazine that aliteracy was, in fact, a much bigger problem in the United States than illiteracy. He writes,

>Most students learn how to read but many do not choose to read. Why should they? Their schools, homes, and communities are bursting with new and exciting television programs, videotapes, movies, and computer games, while a majority of the books in their school library media centers are obsolete and unattractive. [p. 538]

According to Humphrey, the future looks even worse. Later in his article he points out the alarming fact that currently nationwide "approximately one-half of one book per student is purchased each year." He feels that this figure needs to be increased to at least two books per student each year, but "without the availability of new and appealing books," he warns, "the glitzy labyrinth of nonprint media will continue to win the battle with the books." Humphrey's concerns are backed up by the extensive research on reading that is documented in *The Power of Reading: Insights from the Research* by Stephen Krashen. This book shows the importance of a print-rich environment and the need for libraries to provide children with access to books in quiet, comfortable surroundings.

In May 1992, the National Center for Education Statistics published its findings from a major study of factors influencing the literacy achievements of U.S. students in grades 4, 8, and 12 during 1988 and 1990. Following are some of the results of that study, which were reported in *Reading In and Out of School*. As you will see, the center confirms Humphrey's grim predictions for the future of literacy in the United States.

- The amount of reading that students do for school is positively related to their reading achievement . . . . yet, in 1990, 45 percent of the fourth graders . . . reported reading 10 or fewer pages each day in school.
- Despite extensive research suggesting that effective reading instruction includes moving from an overwhelming emphasis on workbooks toward more opportunities for combining reading and writing activities, implementing such recommendations appears to be an extremely slow process.

- Students at all three grade levels demonstrated difficulty in constructing thoughtful responses to questions asking them to elaborate upon or defend their interpretations of what they read. The majority of students' constructed responses indicated a very general understanding of what was read but failed to provide the details and arguments necessary to support their interpretations.
- The frequency of library use in 1990 appeared to decrease as grade level increased. Two-thirds of the fourth graders said they visited the library at least weekly, compared to one-fourth of the eighth graders and 10 percent of the twelfth graders. Most of the eighth graders said they went to the library on a monthly basis, and most twelfth graders reported only yearly use of the library. [pp. 4–7]

The above findings make it clear why "business as usual" in schools today will not produce children who both want to read and can read well.

Principal Harvey vividly remembered the first step she took away from "business as usual" and toward resource-based learning aimed at increasing students' reading abilities. She said that her initial problem was dealing with teachers who were attached to their basal readers. She explained, "Because I wanted to move very slowly, I first said to teachers, 'Every reading plan needs to move beyond the basal some time during the year, and that time should be planned with the media specialist so that she knows what the topic is going to be, can gather materials, and can rearrange her time to work with you and your kids.'"

Harvey has consistently found that once teachers have had a successful experience with resource-based learning by seeing the kinds of activities that children get involved with and by having experienced the support that a media specialist can provide them, they often say, "Well, I'm ready to do that again!" She explained, "It is not so much a matter of dramatically turning away from an old teaching approach—so much as increasingly incorporating a resource-based approach to learning over a period of time."

Whole Language. Across the country the whole language movement—which holds that communication and meaning are the goals of reading, writing, and learning about language—has been one specific educational response to students' reading needs. Whole language teachers, therefore, teach skills not as an end in themselves but as a means of reaching those goals. In practice, one of the goals of this movement is to have children read good literature—rather than abridged and/or watered down versions in readers or—even worse—stories created according to some kind of designated formula for content and ability levels.

Unfortunately, in some schools the spirit of the whole language approach is already being negated in two ways. First, at the very heart of the whole language movement is integration of learning; however, in many cases teachers are using their classroom collections as an excuse to stay in their classrooms. As Director Dobrot exclaimed, "The whole language approach really is backfiring because teachers are becoming self-contained again." As a result, in those situations the scope of students' learning is once again being confined to the four walls of a classroom.

The second and equally insidious result of misusing the whole language approach occurs when teachers have all of their students always read the same literature at the same time. Basically, this practice merely substitutes literature for the old basal readers. Of course, it is more convenient for teachers to have students all reading the same thing at the same time; it is easier for class discussions and tests. However, this approach has some of the same inherent problems that using a basal reader has, i.e., it requires all students to cover the same material at the same time—despite their different interests and their different reading abilities. In such cases, the end result usually is knowledge about some classics, but few educators would accept that as the goal of reading. In *B. J. Skinner: The Man and His Ideas,* written by R. Evans, Skinner is quoted as saying, "We shouldn't teach 'great' books; we should teach a love of reading." Certainly a love of reading is a far more worthwhile goal.

The whole language approach, if properly implemented, can be a major step in the right direction, but only the integration of a wide range of real-world print materials into the curriculum in a resource-based approach to learning will ensure future generations of readers. *(For an excellent summary of research on reading and implications for schooling, read* The Power of Reading: Insights from the Research, *which is listed in the Selected Reading List on page 151.)*

TECHNOLOGY

Whole books have been written about information technology, its capabilities, and its effects on children. Because many Americans love quick fixes, they have looked particularly to technology as a solution to pressing problems. In the 1960s, for example, everyone believed that instructional television was going to be the salvation of education. Not only has television not lived up to this great potential, but it has also become the object of much criticism by educators and parents. However, an objective look at all technologies reveals that none of them are bad in and of themselves. Rather, the challenge is to harness them so that they can become the powerful servants of learning that they have the potential to be.

In order to start reaping the greatest benefits of technology, you need to view it ONLY as a means to an end, not as an end in itself. If harnessed, technology can be a valuable component in resource-based learning for several reasons. First, television, computer networks, CD-ROMs, and other technologies significantly expand the resources available to teachers and media specialists when they are planning learning units; these same resources are available to students when they are preparing and presenting their work. Second, technology can to some degree level the playing field between the have's and have not's by bringing an incredibly rich array of resources to remote and modestly funded schools. Finally, technology can enhance appreciation for people of diverse backgrounds. (The remainder of this chapter will touch briefly upon each of these issues.)

Technology To Serve Learning Needs. Technology plays a major role in resource-based learning because it offers a variety of tools that educators can use to teach any subject to children of diverse backgrounds. Moreover, no one can deny that some technologies are extremely well suited to teaching certain subjects. For example, there are clear advantages to learning to speak a foreign language by means of an audiotape and to practicing math skills by means of a computer. Likewise, while a book is unexcelled at stimulating the imaginations of those who can read with ease, its usefulness in stimulating an appreciation of classical music or in teaching breathing techniques is limited.[1] A child, therefore, who may respond to one medium like a walking zombie may well come alive to another.

Moreover, combining different methods and technologies has long been known to increase learning capacities and retention. As the Cone of Learning, *(see Figure 3.2)* clearly illustrates, students retain only 10 percent of what they read and only 20 percent of what they hear, but their retention rate leaps to 90 percent for what they both say and do.

---

1. Books and journals are considered tools of information technology because both are products of either printing presses or online publishing operations.

FIGURE 3.2

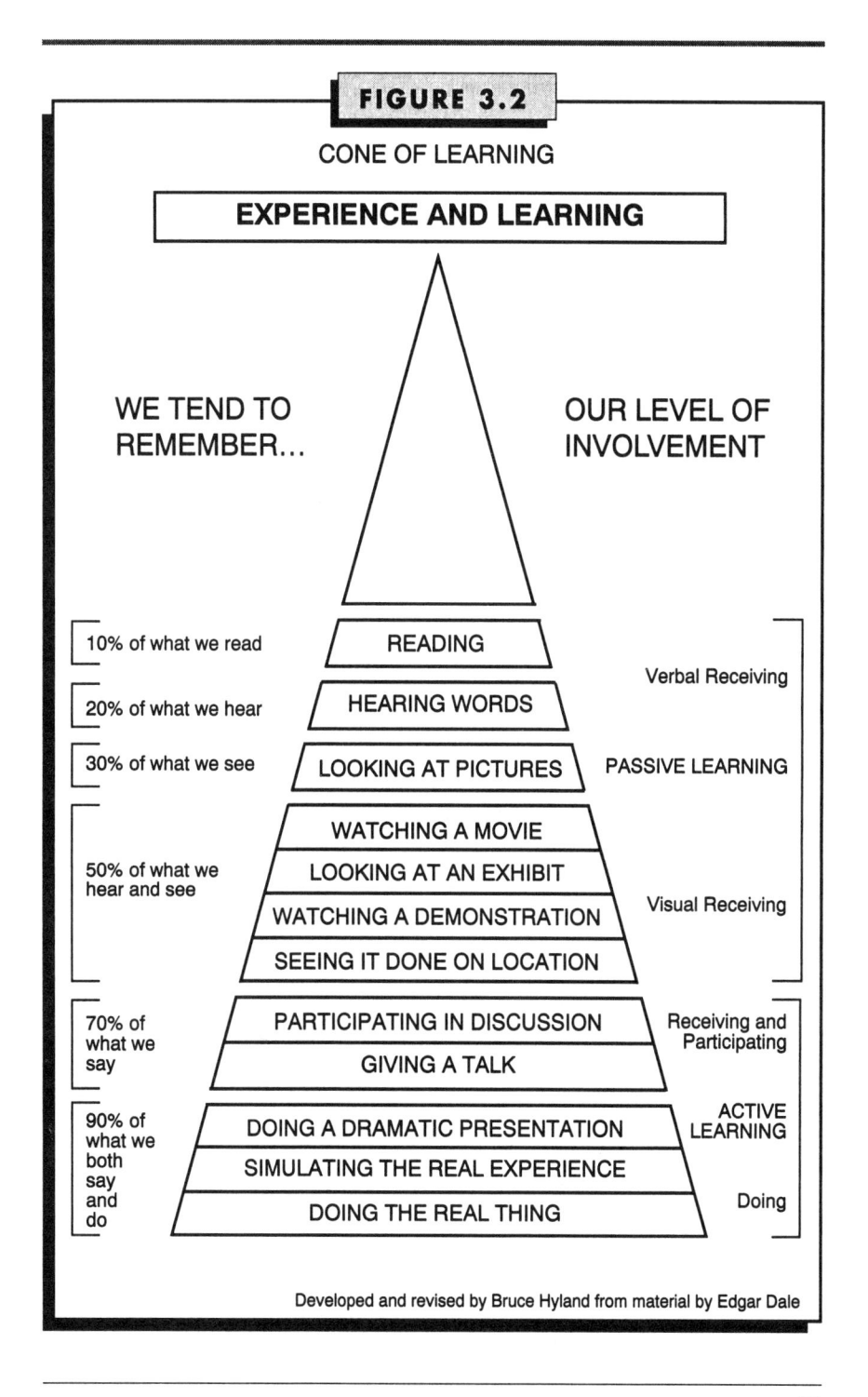

CONE OF LEARNING

EXPERIENCE AND LEARNING

WE TEND TO REMEMBER...

OUR LEVEL OF INVOLVEMENT

We tend to remember	Activity	Level of Involvement
10% of what we read	READING	Verbal Receiving
20% of what we hear	HEARING WORDS	Verbal Receiving
30% of what we see	LOOKING AT PICTURES	PASSIVE LEARNING
50% of what we hear and see	WATCHING A MOVIE	Visual Receiving
	LOOKING AT AN EXHIBIT	
	WATCHING A DEMONSTRATION	
	SEEING IT DONE ON LOCATION	
70% of what we say	PARTICIPATING IN DISCUSSION	Receiving and Participating
	GIVING A TALK	
90% of what we both say and do	DOING A DRAMATIC PRESENTATION	ACTIVE LEARNING
	SIMULATING THE REAL EXPERIENCE	
	DOING THE REAL THING	Doing

Developed and revised by Bruce Hyland from material by Edgar Dale

Technology To Showcase Learning. When students make creative use of technology to produce a product that demonstrates their mastery of the subject, they retain more of what they have learned because the information they produce becomes a part of them. A simple example would be a student's use of a cassette player to record and self-evaluate an oral book report. Many other examples, such as those that follow, involve far more sophisticated technologies.

The first example comes from a third grade class—under the guidance of teacher Kitty Huebler—at the Pot Spring Elementary School in Timonium, MD. For a number of years, the students at this school have been involved with claymation film projects, which have won several prizes at the Maryland State Media Festival and the International Media Festival. In the spring of 1993, the third graders' super-8 film production was "Touring Baltimore with a Dinosaur." In the film a dinosaur, which hatches from a huge egg at the Maryland Science Center, takes a tour of Baltimore with two children who become its friend. As a local newspaper reported, "The children say they learned so much doing research for the project that they decided to fashion a book entitled 'B is for Baltimore' with some of their newly learned facts." More recently the class has begun creating a video with computer-generated graphics.

Huebler explained her students' involvement in this project by saying, "It's education in action. It's just not sitting in a class and learning from a book. The children learn key values, responsibility, art, music, language, and math skills by doing." In January 1993, Huebler, four students, and their parents traveled to New Orleans to receive first prize in the mixed media category at the International Student Media Festival.

The second example deals with the motivational power of television and how it can lead to better reading skills. Some years ago when Shirl Schiffman was the media specialist at an elementary school in Tallahassee, Florida, she discovered some video equipment in a closet. No one remembered how it had gotten there or how long it had been there, but it was hers to use. After talking with students and teachers, she decided to have a weekly news show that highlighted school activities. Any students could be TV newscasters if they were willing to write their scripts and practice reading them aloud.

Three good friends in the fifth grade were particularly excited about the project. Each week the boys carefully researched their stories and wrote their scripts. After a few shows, however, it became clear that one of the three was not doing as well as his friends because he was a poor reader. Schiffman discussed this problem with the reading teacher, who was delighted to finally find something the boy wanted to read. After she worked with him on his scripts, his reading level jumped several grade levels.

In both of these examples, video/film production generated enthusiasm for projects that included "painless" research, integration of information from a variety of sources, and final products that resulted in great pride for all involved. Clearly, then, information technologies in general—and video in particular—are valuable not only as sources of information but also as vehicles for displaying what has been learned across the curriculum.

Technology To Build Bridges. Technology can link children with other children halfway around the world and with resources far beyond those of their particular communities—thereby expanding the children's cultural and social awareness. One example of this benefit of technology comes from the Western Technology Dream Project, which was launched in 1991 through a collaborative effort of the National Education Association, the American Association of School Administrators, and the American Association of School

Librarians. The goal of the program was to give technology to 15 schools from Oregon to Iowa so that they could obtain a stated educational "dream."

The U.S. West Foundation first provided a seed grant of $80,000 to establish this project, enabling educators to make radical restructuring of schools a reality and to demonstrate the power of technology to the public and the media. Among those responding to the challenge to "Send Us Your Dream" of how students' educations could be improved through technology were two very different schools with a common problem. Both the Arapahoe School District #38, located on the remote Wind River Indian Reservation in Wyoming, and the Corvelia Elementary School in Edina, Minnesota, wanted their students to experience cultures other than their own. Students at the Arapahoe school had no contact with non-Native American students, and they wanted to interact with society outside the reservation and to develop the skills needed to cope with U.S. society as a whole. Because travel was expensive and inconvenient, communications technology seemed to be the school's best solution. Meanwhile, the students in Edina suffered from their own upper-middle-class brand of isolation.

Following are excerpts from a June 14, 1992, article in the *Washington Post,* which describes what happened when the Wyoming students linked up with yet another group of students in Sioux Falls, South Dakota.

> The other day, Native American youngsters at Arapahoe School near Riverton, Wyoming, chatted by television satellite with suburban youngsters at Whittier Middle School in Sioux Falls, South Dakota. For an hour, technology bridged the miles between the two schools and the students bridged gaps created by different histories and cultures . . . .
>
> After overcoming their initial shyness, the students used the outer space television satellite to ask each other down-to-earth questions. One Whittier student

asked an Arapahoe youngster, "Would you rather be called *Indians* or *Native Americans?*" The answer: "Native American." The kids discussed haircuts, food, after-school sports, Native American traditions, and a host of other things.

They shared opinions about the Los Angeles riots. If people from different races could talk to and learn to understand each other—as they themselves were doing—the radical hostility that fed the tragedy in Los Angeles could be avoided, the students said . . . .

Seventh grader Claudette Duran of Arapahoe, who explained her tribal name means "Woman Who Brings in the Morning Water," said she learned "you can communicate with anyone in the world without feeling guilty." Whittier 7th grader Arianne Sorretta told the Sioux Falls *Argus Leader* that the session showed if you talk "face to face," you find out people are good and "you don't have such negative thoughts."

The Western Technology Dream Project has set a good model for having educational needs and challenges drive the use of technology—rather than starting with technology and then trying to get people to do something with it.

NATIONAL EDUCATION GOALS

By now most concerned educators have read the National Education Goals as well as the four strategy tracks identified by the Bush administration in *American 2000: An Education Strategy*. The goals are expected to continue to be the national focus for education reform because President Clinton was involved in their development while he was governor of Arkansas. *(For ease of reference, the National Education Goals and the four strategy tracks are contained in Appendix C on page 178.)*

Libraries for the National Education Goals, an ERIC publication, describes how school library media centers and public libraries are contributing to the accomplishment of the national goals and supporting the prescribed strategies. Rather than duplicating a portion of this easily available document, it seems more helpful to share the results of related research that was completed by Christina S. Doyle in 1992. Doyle used a research technique that involved a panel of experts, some of whom came from the National Forum on Information Literacy, which is an umbrella group made up of over 60 broad-based national organizations committed to empowering individuals through information literacy. *(For the list of member organizations, see Appendix D on page 179.)* In the executive summary of her research, which she prepared for the Forum, Doyle reports the panel's consensus on how information literacy relates to the National Education Goals. In addition, she goes on to identify possible outcome measures. For the sake of time and space, only some of the outcome measures are highlighted here; however, her entire summary for Goal III is reprinted in Appendix E on page 180.

Goal III is singled out for two reasons. First, it has an integral relationship to resource-based learning in schools because of its emphasis on being prepared for further learning. Second, this goal—along with Goal V—addresses needed workforce skills, which have increasingly become a topic of concern to employers and educators alike. For example, in the November/December 1992 issue of *Change,* Peter Cappeli, co-director of the National Center on the Educational Quality of the Workforce at the University of Pennsylvania and a professor at the Wharton School of Business, summarizes the requirements determined by virtually every system of job analysis.

All of the items on his list complement Goals III and V because of their emphasis on students being able "to use their minds well so they may be prepared for . . . further learning and productivity in our modern economy" and on students acquiring "the knowledge and skills necessary to compete in a

global economy." Moreover, the demands businesses are making, some of which are listed below, are proven outcomes of resource-based learning programs.
- interpersonal skills
- communications, both oral and written
- critical thinking, broadly defined (problem solving, reasoning, and so forth)
- motivation and other personal attitudinal characteristics
- working with data and information
- math skills

Goal III states:

> American students will leave grades four, eight, and twelve having demonstrated competency in challenging subject matter including English, mathematics, science, history, and geography; and every school in America will ensure that all students learn to use their minds well, so they may be prepared for responsible citizenship, further learning, and productive employment in our modern economy.

Included in Doyle's summary of the experts' consensus regarding actions that schools can undertake to achieve Goal III are the following.
- School goals will assure that information literacy skills are included across all curricular areas, so that all students apply information literacy as they learn the underlying principles of each curricular area.
- Sites will develop curricular objectives that include information literacy across all curricular disciplines in the context of basic principles that are inherent to a particular subject area.
- Sites will develop curricular assessment methods that include alternative assessment procedures such as projects, portfolios, and performances and integrate the information literacy process.
- Critical thinking/problem solving skills will be developed and honed through meaningful activities involving finding and interpreting information.

Beyond efforts at the national level to bring the power of resource-based learning to bear upon achieving the National Education Goals, similar endeavors at the state level are also underway to address state endorsed adaptations of the goals. Colorado, for example, has produced a document entitled "Implementing the Colorado State Board of Education Goals through School Library Media Programs." *(This document is reprinted in its entirety in Appendix F on page 182.)*

Given, then, the close relationship between information literacy and the accomplishment of key National Education Goals, state adaptations of the latter, and the demands of the workforce, promoting resource-based learning would certainly seem a wise course to persue.

CHAPTER 4

OVERCOMING BARRIERS

> "Ultimately you have to do what is right for the kids."
>
> ALAN THORMEYER, PRINCIPAL
> OF THE CLEARSPRING
> ELEMENTARY SCHOOL, DAMASCUS, MD

TAKE SOME TIME TO ANSWER THE FOLLOWING QUESTIONS because your answers will help you assess your school's readiness to move toward resource-based learning. Also, thoughtfully examining some key areas that impact on resource-based learning will help you understand some possible barriers to its successful implementation. (Those barriers are discussed in this chapter.)

- Visit your library media center and observe how the students spend their time. Do they seem engrossed in their activities? Look at the expressions on their faces. Do most seem eager and enthusiastic or bored and passive?
- How attractive is your media center? How up-to-date, varied, and extensive are all of the collections?
- What activities consume most of the library media specialist's time?
- How much collaborative learning is already going on in your school? How easily and under what circumstances can groups of teachers get together and plan curriculum both by themselves and with the media specialist?

- Finally, through informal conversations, how would you assess the ability of your school's personnel to respond to the idea of more fully integrating library resources into the classroom curriculum?

Now you should have a sense of your school's readiness to move from a more or less traditional approach to teaching to one based upon the broadest possible integration of real-world information resources. As with any new endeavor, there are some potential barriers that can impede progress and even stop it altogether. However, if you are steadfast to a vision of the ultimate benefits of resource-based learning, all these barriers become surmountable.

Although every elementary school is different, there are four significant barriers that you could face when implementing resource-based learning at your school. They are listed below in their order of importance; however, the different issues actually overlap.

1. fixed library schedules
2. staff resistance
3. inadequate resources
4. impatience

Fixed Library Schedules

Picture the following scene: In your capacity as principal, you have just visited a newly opened public library in your neighborhood. You are delighted with the inviting atmosphere, the obvious dedication and competence of the staff, and the availability of a wide range of up-to-date information resources. When you go home that evening and describe the new library, you generate such enthusiasm that you and your family plan an outing to the library on Friday afternoon.

When Friday arrives, everyone is ready to go. Each

family member has her or his own agenda. You plan to meet the librarian in charge of school relations and discuss possible cooperative activities as well as check out the mystery collection. Your wife wants to begin planning a family vacation in New England as well as get some books on home solar energy projects. Your teenage daughter has to research a speech on the invention of lasers, and she also wants to start checking out colleges. Your younger child can hardly wait to see the puppet theater you had previously described to her.

Imagine, however, how you would feel if a guard stopped your family at the front door and questioned your eligibility to enter. When you give your address, he tells you that people from your block do not have library privileges except on Wednesday mornings between nine and ten o'clock. You object, of course, saying that time slot is out of the question because your children must be in school and you and your spouse must be at work. Nevertheless, as the guard continues to block the doorway, he informs you that in order to ensure that everyone has equal access to the library, the schedule must be honored. When you protest again, reminding the guard that you are a taxpayer and have the right to use the library whenever you need to get information, he explains that limited resources necessitate some inconvenience for everyone. He suggests that if Friday afternoon between four and five o'clock is the best time for you and your family, you could try to switch times with the people who are scheduled for that hour. On the surface this scenario might seem totally ridiculous, but it may actually be taking place in your school right now if your library media center has a fixed schedule.

Although fixed library scheduling is intended to give all students regular access to the library media center, it actually puts students' learning needs last because it prevents a natural flow from a need or an interest to information gathering and most often leaves students high and dry, like fish out of water. Fixed schedules also do not allow for any serendipity in learning. The schedule, in fact, is given more importance than the learners, and this distressing fact is antithetical to both resource-based learning and to the students' preparation for lifelong learning. Indeed, when they are not allowed to establish a pattern of behavior of first identifying an information need and then following through by seeking the information amidst an open universe of resources, students are deprived of developing a basic survival skill necessary for success in the increasing complexities of this Information Age.

Although staff resistance is covered in more depth in the next section of this chapter, it needs to be pointed out here that many teachers resist the elimination of a fixed library schedule because traditionally during the time when their students are in the library each week, they can work on curriculum development or planning. In other words, student library time has meant free work time for teachers.

Principal Rhodes pointed out that there is another more complex reason why teachers sometimes resist giving up fixed library schedules. She said, "The fixed schedule is a security blanket that some teachers try to hang on to because of their resistance simply to change." She went on to explain that the time students spend in the library is a reprieve to teachers. She continued, "They can bring their class to the library and then have some time to catch up on grading or to catch up on whatever. They look forward to that period in the library so they can let their hair down or feel 'I am not responsible.'" Rhodes cautioned, "Now if you take that away and say they also have to become a part of the library learning process—that they cannot be passive anymore—you have not only taken away something from the teachers, but you have also required them to spend extra time planning with the library media specialist!"

Although many obstacles can interfere with the quality of resource-based learning, fixed library scheduling is most damaging of them all. Fortunately, it is an obstacle that is totally under a principal's control. A certain amount of creativity, of course, is helpful when moving a staff from fixed schedules to flexible schedules, and careful exploration with teachers will often turn up a variety of options for providing free periods other than library times. Some planned activities, such as an older class adopting a younger one to work on a particular project, lend themselves naturally to a combined class that can be managed by one teacher and an aide—thus providing the second teacher with some free time. Some other possibilities might center around academic, cultural, or athletic events such as an ongoing intramural program. In addition, classes might be combined to plan a schoolwide event or a program for an upcoming PTO meeting. Another option might be an innovative use of teacher aides or volunteers for study and/or work sessions that have been preplanned by the classroom teacher. This last option is discussed more fully in the next chapter.

Sometimes teachers are not the only ones who are concerned when fixed library schedules are changed over to flexible schedules. Often parents will worry that their children will not read as much if they cannot check out a different book each week. Director Dobrot, who has dealt with this problem, stated, "Our argument is—if you force the children to go into the library media center every week for 20 or 30 minutes to get a book, they're going to grab any book—whether it's good or not—and then the book will usually stay in their bookbag unread until they come back the following week. However, if the books they check out are tied to what they are learning, the children will actually end up reading more because they'll really want to read the books!"

TEACHER RESISTANCE

Resistance to change is not unusual. Most people get very comfortable in their normal routines, and if things are going fairly well, there is little motivation to change. In education the lack of major problems may almost be a deterrent to change, since the need to make improvements may not be as clear as it is in schools where students perform significantly below the norm on standardized tests or other measurements of success.

Some elementary teachers also may resent resource-based learning because it breaks down the security of isolation that surrounds them. Indeed, resource-based learning requires that teachers work collaboratively, first with the school library media specialist and then with each other. To some teachers, this prospect may be uncomfortable and even threatening. However, schools where collaborative learning projects have been implemented show surprisingly positive results: not only are students having more fun learning, but teachers are having more fun teaching!

Information Specialist Carter (Sands) addressed the process of breaking down teacher isolation when she said, "Although it is threatening for some teachers to come out from the isolation of their classrooms, I find that once they come out—however that happens and it happens in a variety of ways—they like it." She added, "Some, of course, may not stay out, but if they go back, they will come out again. The more positive experiences they have, the more willing and ready they are to come out again."

Dean Pacholl, a retired elementary school media specialist from Austin, Minnesota, explained that he had undertaken a progressive plan to break down teacher resistance to resource-based learning at his school. Following is his account of the plan and its results.

In order to overcome resistance, several steps were taken. First, I established a committee composed of parents, teachers, the building principal, and myself. We studied the concept of resource-based/integrated instruction, attended workshops, visited other media centers, surveyed professional literature, and invited resource persons to meet with us. As a result, in the buildings where resource-based learning/integrated instruction had the support of the building principal and parents, we were able to establish a pilot program in grades 3–5.

After one year of trial and continued committee involvement, the building principal provided release time for teachers to meet with me, at grade levels, to select and plan integrated units of instruction which they were willing to plan, teach, and evaluate. After the first year, teachers were beginning to see the benefits of resource-based learning/integrated instruction and flexible scheduling. As a result, the following year we opened up the selection of units of instruction to permit individual teachers to select and plan units of their choice with the media specialist. Now two units of instruction are required at each grade level, with additional units chosen by individual teachers or grade levels.

There still are teachers who resist the concept of resource-based learning/integrated instruction and flexible scheduling, but the number is decreasing each year.

Looking ahead, Information Specialist Carter (Sands) projects that in the near future, teachers will not be able to choose whether or not to resist. She stressed, "Collaboration is too critical to everything in education and in terms of both the work world and global culture. If you listen to what is happening out there, business people are saying that it is not those with the best ideas who are going to win in the future; rather, the winners will be those who have the best coalitions." She concluded by pointing out that the American dream has always been based on an individual's having a goal and persevering toward it. "That is still important," she stressed, "but you can't do it as an individual anymore because our whole culture is in the process of change!"

The real challenge, then, for you and other principals is to find ways to encourage collaborative efforts among library media specialists and teachers or, at least, to create an environment that is conducive to cooperation. One approach Principal Dangremond took was to fund all activities that involved resource-based learning. In her interview she said, "To encourage teachers, I told them that if they were doing a project or a unit with the media specialist, then I would provide additional funds for any kind of support materials they would need."

As other incentives, some principals showcased resource-based learning programs and praised them at PTO and school board meetings. Even displaying collaborative learning projects and encouraging students to present their research to other classes can serve as incentives. Principals Dangremond and Thormeyer also stated that they are willing to take over classes so that their teachers can spend uninterrupted time planning with the library media specialist. Thormeyer also stressed that whatever tactics a principal takes, not everyone will be pleased. As a result, he said, "You may have to force some issues, sometimes, and if you do, you'll probably cause some unhappiness to the staff; however, ultimately you have to do what is right for the kids."

Although you should never underestimate the impact of teacher resistance on the launching of a resource-based program at your school, you also should not assume that you will get resistance from all teachers. Even initially you probably will receive the enthusiastic support of many good teachers because resource-based learning will make good sense to them.

Recently, Christopher M. Clark, a professor of educational psychology at Michigan State University, created a composite of a good teacher based on his in-depth study. He summarized his findings in the January/February 1993 issue of *Doubts & Certainties,* a publication of the National Education Association National Center for Innovation. Following are a few excerpts from that article.

> In the end, good teachers equip their students for confident, independent thought and action in an uncertain world. Good teachers prepare [students] for a world of difference. Good teachers know when to let [students] go. And this is almost always before [they] feel ready to be on [their] own. [p. 1]
>
> In the words of children, good teachers nurture students by treating them as intelligent people who can become even more intelligent, taking the time to learn who they are and what they love, treating them fairly by treating them differently. [p. 4]

The teachers on your staff who fit these descriptions will not resist your invitation to resource-based learning because they will understand the value of creating independent learners; in fact, they probably will be among your staunchest defenders and supporters.

INADEQUATE RESOURCES

Concern about additional costs often sets off warning alarms and gets principals thinking of all the reasons why they cannot incorporate a resource-based approach to learning at their schools. In fact, tight budgets are usually seen as THE barrier. It is true that successful resource-based learning programs will cause teachers and media specialists to want more information resources, a broader range of mediums, and more technology for their students. Indeed, principals acknowledged the importance of both the size and the nature of the collection. However, with creative leadership, limited financial resources do not have to be a significant barrier to launching and maintaining a successful program of resource-based learning—even in these times of tight budgets.

Chapter 5, entitled "Your Investment," describes in more detail how to garner and reallocate resources and technology to support resource-based learning in your school. For now, however, you can rest assured that funding will not be your most formidable barrier because it is always more difficult to change habits and attitudes than it is to obtain or reallocate financial resources.

IMPATIENCE

It is important to state at the start that changing over to resource-based learning takes time. A number of those interviewed stated, for example, that it takes at least three to five years—or even longer—to totally implement resource-based learning. Of course, the time needed will vary from school to school depending on the resources available and the commitment of the personnel involved. Principal Dangremond, warned about the temptation to move too quickly. "After I had attended an elementary principals' conference that dealt with group dynamics and decision making," she said, "I knew that some confusion and anxiety were a normal part of the change-over process. However, I personally found it very difficult to be patient and not rush the process." She went on to explain, "I had to remember that not all teachers are risk takers; they are not all immediately enthusiastic about new ideas—particularly when I could not hand them a tested, proven package." However, emphasizing the rewards of such patience, Library Media Specialist Coatney said, "It has taken five years to get this school to the point where the teachers and I plan monthly, but it has been worth the wait!"

Also commenting on the fact that difficulties often slow down the results of resource-based learning, Diane Skorupski, the library media specialist at the Liberty Elementary School in Tucson, Arizona, compared her experiences to a Ziggy cartoon she had once seen. She said, "I once saw a cartoon in which Ziggy is bowling. He has a hopeful expression on his face as he releases the ball, but then his expression becomes worried a few frames later as the ball comes careening back toward him!" She added, "I have felt like Ziggy so often as I have attempted to be creative and innovative, but I have kept up my struggle to bring my faculty from the Dark Ages into the renaissance of 21st century library resource centers!"

Like Skorupski, many others have forged ahead in spite of barriers and obstacles. Writing in the Winter 1993 issue of *Taproot: Journal of the New Hampshire Educational Media Association,* Ellen Tirone, the media specialist at the Harold Martin School in Contoocook, New Hampshire, spoke for so many when she wrote,

> It would have been so easy to be sidetracked by our roadblocks: a half-time library media professional, outcome uncertainty, individuals' resistance, scheduling dilemmas, and traditional notions. Bound by common interest in meeting our students' needs, we worked through initial barriers and have promoted an enthusiasm for learning and a sense of accomplishment . . . Our risk taking has been rewarded in many ways, both tangible and intangible. The Harold Martin School staff embraces change, still cautiously, but with a sense of confidence, knowing what can result.

STAFF DEVELOPMENT

Staff development is so essential that nothing else in this book matters very much if there are not adequate in-service and other developmental opportunities for school personnel. Indeed, a staff development day called by the superintendent of schools of the Blue Valley School District in Overland

Park, Kansas, started the whole movement toward resource-based learning in that district. On that occasion, consultants met for a day with the principals and their library media specialists to define and discuss what an outstanding library media program really is. As Library Media Specialist Coatney reported,

> Before the end of the day, we had each principal and library media specialist team meet with each one of the consultants. Emphasizing the fact that the library media program was going to be a part of every subject area, they designed the program they were going to have the next year to enrich the curriculum. At the end of the day, the principals and the library media specialists voted for it. So there was a real buy-in!

Similarly, the amount of staff development opportunities available to teachers may be the one factor that most influences the length of time required to firmly establish a resource-based learning program in your school. Principal Harvey listed staff development among the three most crucial elements for a successful program; in fact, the importance of such efforts was a recurring theme in all the other interviews as well. As you consider the following staff development options you could adapt to meet your school's particular needs, think about the two major goals that sufficient staff development should accomplish: (1) teachers will know how to proceed; and (2) they will gain the confidence needed to proceed successfully.

Self-Generated. Good staff development does not have to be burdensome or even costly. For example, one of the best in-service sessions possible could result from turning the meeting over to teachers on your staff—or teachers from a nearby school—who are enthusiastic about resource-based learning and who are willing to share their recent success stories. Teachers and library media specialists also value other less formal situations in which they can share their successes and failures with resource-based learning and brainstorm ideas for effective approaches or methods.

In addition, some carefully chosen articles or books can serve as the basis for productive discussions. Also consider using materials like the recently published workshop guide entitled *Beyond Flexible Scheduling*. This book is an excellent source of material on which several in-service training sessions could be based. The guide, which was created by Nancy Dobrot and Rosemary McCawley, an elementary school media specialist and a teacher, respectively, offers a practical approach for implementing a resource-based learning program and for facilitating staff development efforts. *(For more information about this publication, see the Selected Reading List on page 150.)*

Similar materials that more directly relate to particular needs in your area can also be developed by pooling resources within a school district. For example, a group of eight Chapter 1 schools in Los Angeles cooperated in preparing a similar type of resource book to support staff development activities for their school personnel, parents, and students.

State Generated. In some states, the department of education and/or the state library can provide you with staff training opportunities that are geared to both teachers and library media specialists. The Colorado State Board of Education, for example, lists criteria regarding library media programs in its publication "Rules for the Administration of the Accreditation of School Districts." Following is an excerpt from that publication.

Each school district shall provide:
- A library media program that reflects the diversity of American society;
- All students with equitable access to current print, non-print, and electronic resources for use in resource-based learning;

- Evidence that students demonstrate information skills and proficiencies which include the use of technology.

To facilitate the fulfillment of these criteria, the Colorado State Board of Education offers workshops across the state for school personnel. Moreover, it has many handouts covering areas such as the development of a library media program, the promotion of a dialogue about resource-based learning among teachers, and the development of instructional action plans with measurable outcomes.

Pennsylvania, on the other hand, has been moving toward an outcome-based approach to education in which students' success will be measured by what they have learned as opposed to how much time they have spent in school or what subjects they have covered. To prepare school personnel—particularly library media specialists—to respond thoroughly to such outcomes as information literacy and the use of information technology, the Pennsylvania State Library has regularly provided pertinent information to school personnel, prepared training packages, and offered conference programs.

For several years now, Susan C. Snider, the curriculum supervisor of library media services at the New Hampshire State Department of Education, has also been providing an extensive staff-development program. Following, for example, is a sampling of the many offerings available to state administrators, teachers, and media specialists.

> Between November 1988 and March 1991, at least 50 percent (over 100) of the library media generalists in the state attended at least one all-day seminar, with either an administrator or a classroom teacher, in the area of information skills and resource-based learning (RBL). A smaller number have taken advantage of the more extensive training in the "how-to's" of RBL. In the summer of 1989, about 17 teams of library professionals and teachers attended a three-day seminar on collaborative program planning and

teaching. Between January 1991 and January 1992, 15 teams of library media generalists and health educators participated in a project that involved the development of resource-based learning units for HIV/AIDS education. Extensive training for resource-based curriculum development was also a part of the project.

Besides state government offerings, some state professional organizations also provide training programs. For example, in the spring of 1992, the Illinois School Library Media Organization sponsored back-to-back conferences on information literacy and resource-based learning. Teams consisting of a superintendent of schools, a school library media specialist, and a public librarian were invited to the first day of the conference; and representatives from state teacher organizations (the Illinois Teachers of English, the Illinois Teachers of Math, and so on) were invited the second day. During both days the issue of how resource-based learning could help address the educational priorities of the participants was discussed, and both days provided opportunities for dialogue between people who had previously not networked to accomplish shared educational goals.

The purpose of listing these examples is to stress that when you are looking for resources to support staff development, first look at what is available locally; then look beyond your own professional contacts. In other words, make sure you take advantage of whatever materials and training resources are available to you at little or no cost from state agencies and library related professional organizations. However, if no such resources are available in your state, you and your library media specialist should begin questioning why they are not available and articulating the need for them.

In-Service for Parents. Finally, you also may need to arrange for some training sessions for parents who may initially be concerned about why their children are spending less time memorizing facts and more time working on group projects. Most schools changing to resource-based learning have found, however, that such a need will be short lived because parents quickly become aware of their children's increased enthusiasm about school, and they are usually pleased with the products of their children's integrated resource-based units.

In summary, it is impossible to overestimate the importance of in-service training and other means of teacher development. Even with a clearly articulated vision, a well equipped center, and a talented and dedicated library media specialist, success will be elusive if teachers do not feel empowered to give students access to real-world resources.

CHAPTER 5
YOUR INVESTMENT

> **"**Most important is a library media specialist who has a vision . . ."
>
> SUSAN DANGREMOND, PRINCIPAL OF
> THE LAKEVIEW ELEMENTARY SCHOOL, HOLLAND, MI

IN THESE DAYS OF BELT TIGHTENING AND BUDGET CUTS, the good news is that your school can make remarkable progress toward resource-based learning without spending any additional money. Of course, as you witness the successes of this approach to learning, you will likely find yourself wanting to reallocate some of your resources to better support it.

STAFFING

The first question you need to address concerning staffing is not "How many staff members should I have in the library media center?" but rather "How qualified are my staff members?" and "How are they spending their time?". Once these questions are answered, then you need to take the time to analyze whether or not you need any additional staff.

Library Media Specialist. Whether you need to spend any additional money to develop resource-based learning depends, of course, on whether you have a good library media specialist on your staff—one who can move beyond the caretaking functions that once characterized a librarian's job. Principal Dangremond, whose words began this chapter, articulated this need from first-hand experience. She said,

> Most important is a library media specialist who has a vision, one who communicates well, one who works collaboratively with teachers, and one who has both technological knowledge and knowledge of the curriculum. In other words, the media specialist needs to be a master teacher.

Therefore, at the very outset of any resource-based undertaking, you will need to ask yourself whether or not your media specialist is capable—perhaps with some staff development opportunities—of becoming a dynamic team player in curriculum development. If not, you may have to make a change in personnel.

In all likelihood, however, your library media specialist will enthusiastically respond to your interest in resource-based learning. Retired library media specialist Pacholl expressed just such a response when he wrote, "I had been in media for 22 years, but the last five years—since my school adopted resource-based/integrated instruction—were the most exciting and rewarding years of my career. I feel now that I was making a vital, important contribution to the educational process."

Your media specialist should not only be "good"; he or she should also be full-time. Many of those interviewed warned against dividing a media specialist among several schools. Library Media Coordinator van Deusen, for example, stressed that if her school system had one media specialist for five schools, she would put the media specialist in one school and let the other four schools go without. She explained by saying, "I really believe in depth, not breath. If you have one person spread out among five schools, he or she is not going to be able to do anything but touch base. A media specialist's time has to be more concentrated than that if you ever want to get a resource-based program off the ground."

If you already have a good full-time library media specialist on your staff, then the next issue you need to address is whether that person is being fully used. Historically, in the pre-Information Age days, librarians were often seen only as babysitters for classes during teachers' prep periods. Chapter 3, however, points out that resource-based learning cannot be successfully implemented with this traditional attitude toward libraries and librarians. Today library media specialists, especially those involved in resource-based learning, must become information specialists, teachers, and instructional partners. (Figure 5.1 on page 74 shows these three major areas of responsibilities of a library media specialist.)

Aides and/or Volunteers. If your school library media specialist is to perform the functions described on Figure 5.1, his or her time must be "rescued" from much of the housekeeping routines that are a part of any library's daily operation—routines such as checking materials in and out, shelving books, and keeping equipment serviced. Freeing the media specialist's time usually requires the combined help of a support staff, volunteers, and perhaps even some student helpers.

Information Specialist Carter (Sands), for example, described why she used parent volunteers to help her with her daily chores. She said, "I needed a lot of help from volunteers because it was not uncommon for me to come into my library and see stacks of books waiting to be checked in or to be put back on the shelves because tasks like those were not my priority. My priority was teaching and working with the kids and the teachers." While recruiting and training volunteers takes time in and of itself, there is definitely a long-range payoff in freeing library media specialists to spend their time in more productive pursuits.

FIGURE 5.1

LIBRARY MEDIA SPECIALIST OF THE 1990s

is a nurturing, caring, and enabling person who fulfills the roles of:

Information Specialist

- makes resources available
- provides access through accurate and efficient retrieval system
- assists users of information available inside and outside media center
- provides access throughout day
- informs users of new materials, equipment, and services
- updates professional skills
- promotes library media program
- promotes a lifelong love of reading and learning

Teacher

- supports curriculum through information skills development
- works jointly with staff in planning instruction
- instructs users
- assists users in media access to outside sources
- provides a variety of media
- informs users of laws and policies in use of materials and information
- encourages parent involvement and participation
- promotes a lifelong love of reading and learning

Instructional Partner

- participates in and accesses major curriculum projects
- offers assistance to users
- assists in assessment, evaluation, and implementation of information
- demonstrates effective use of instructional technologies
- promotes a lifelong love of reading and learning

Developed by the Grand Haven School District, Grand Haven, MI

Library Media Specialist Coatney, who sometimes has between 25 and 30 volunteers helping her, recruits them during school registration. To make sure that the time and expense of training pay off, she lets them choose what they want to do. For example, some like to shelve books, others like to work on art projects and displays, and some always want to work with the children. "I talk to the volunteers a lot about how important they are," she explained, "but I also ask them not to sign up if they can't come in on some kind of schedule." She added, "By taking this approach, I let them see that volunteering for me can't be just a come-in-if-you-can activity, because I really can't run the library without them!"

Several library media specialists also pointed out that parent volunteers are as good as—and sometimes better than—a newsletter for reporting to other parents on all of the enthusiastic interactive learning that takes place in the library media center. Parent volunteers not only explain what goes on, but they also often generate an enormous amount of interest and support. *(For more information about recruiting volunteers and using them effectively, see Chapter 6.)*

COLLECTIONS

One of the first steps in preparing for a move to resource-based learning is to have your library media specialist take a survey of your school's collections. To begin such a task, he or she might consider the following evaluative checklist, which is found in *Information Power*. It lists the basic criteria for evaluating the resources needed to support resource-based learning.

- Does the collection support and enhance specific courses and units of instruction taught in the schools?

- For any unit of instruction is/are there
  —a variety of media?
  —materials that are current?
  —enough materials for the number of users?
  —materials that span reading, viewing, listening, and comprehension levels?
  —materials that span the opinion/cultural/political spectrum, if required?
  —materials of interest to students? [p. 78]

The importance of a professional library media specialist in shaping a collection that supports student achievement is documented in a 1992 report by the Colorado Department of Education. The study, which was funded in part by a U.S. Department of Education research grant, studied the positive impact of library media centers on student performance in 221 Colorado public schools during the 1988–1989 school year. Following are some findings of that report.

> The instructional role of the library media specialist shapes the collection and, in turn, academic achievement. A library media center should be staffed by an endorsed library media specialist who is involved not only in identifying materials suitable for school curricula, but also in collaborating with teachers and others in developing curricula. These activities require that the media specialists have adequate support staff. This involvement in the instructional process helps to shape a larger—and, presumably, more appropriate—local collection. [p. 96]

Once the collections have been assessed, your library media specialist should start making plans that utilize them to their maximum. Of course, such optimum utilization can be accomplished only if the teachers and the library media specialist have sufficient time and interest to work together on curriculum planning. If they are jointly planning integrated curriculum projects, they can create assignments that most effectively foster understanding of the subject matter and information literacy.

Although every school can probably make better and more integrated use of the learning materials already available, the need for support materials will grow as more in-depth resource-based learning units are planned. Principal Harvey, speaking generally, commented on the need to make some changes in the media center's collection "so that it really does fit the kinds of teaching that resource-based learning will produce." Ruth Bell, director of Library Media Services for the Blue Valley School District in Overland Park, Kansas, also pointed out that some schools may need to upgrade their library collections with "a heavy emphasis on nonfiction so that the new materials will enrich the school's curriculum."

Eventually, as more and more of the curriculum is transformed into a resource-based learning approach, more creative efforts to provide access to resources will be required. Some possible avenues of expansion are discussed later in this chapter, but even carrying out those suggestions may not provide the richness in materials—particularly multimedia materials—that you may need or want.

Following, therefore, is a suggestion that is well worth considering. If a whole district is committed to resource-based learning or if two or more schools in the region have similar commitments, some arrangements might be made for joint funding of in-depth collections around selected subject/project areas. For example, cooperative planning could lead to the identification of a number of themes—such as weather, pioneers, space exploration, and the environment—on which all of the participating schools would want to base major resource-based learning units. Agreement could be reached on the materials to be purchased for each unit, and then the total cost could be equitably distributed among the schools. The enriched collections could then be rotated among the schools according to a preestablished schedule.

Clearly this approach requires a number of ingredients to make it workable. Planning time is essential, for instance, as are operational guidelines for the schools' responsibilities for lost or damaged materials. In addition, all the schools would have to understand that with resource-based learning, a rotating collection can never be a substitute for a well rounded permanent collection. However, enriched rotating collections can be a very cost-effective way of significantly increasing your school's resources for supporting major learning projects.

Equipment

Although most schools have been caught up in the rush toward technology, many of them have been underutilizing it. Before considering buying new equipment, therefore, take a hard look at how much use your school makes of the technologies it does possess, and then determine how such use could be better integrated into all classes and all subject areas. For example, you may decide that simply moving computers out of the math and science labs and into the library media center and providing in-service training for teachers could significantly increase the use of this equipment. Indeed, making equipment easily accessible and training people to use it are two of the the most important factors in making sure that equipment is used. The third factor is having a school library media specialist who regularly brings to teachers' attention software and classroom applications that match their curriculum needs.

In order to get the most for your investment, your decisions to purchase new equipment—both hardware and software—should also be based on its potential for schoolwide use and the availability of appropriate software for various disciplines. To help in the decision-making process, (or to make the process even more confusing) databases of K–12 resources are increasingly becoming available. For example, the Eisenhower

National Clearinghouse for Mathematics and Science Education will soon produce a multimedia database of K–12 math and science lesson plans and other teaching information. Meanwhile, realizing how difficult it is to adequately access information on curriculum related materials, the Association of Supervision and Curriculum Development, a member of the National Forum on Information Literacy, is committed to becoming "the court of first resort on information resources for decision makers in curriculum and technology."

Cooperative planning of the curriculum by both school library media specialists and teachers will provide a schoolwide perspective on equipment needs. However, because they keep up with information on curriculum related software, library media specialists are in the best position to determine the range and quality of software that can be used on equipment being considered for purchase. Moreover, because of their concern for the entire curriculum, library media specialists can more objectively evaluate the overall impact of decisions about the purchase and use of both hardware and software.

You may also want to consider asking local businesses to donate new or used equipment. For example, the Clearspring Elementary School in Damascus, Maryland, having formed a partnership with GTE, is currently using one of the company's experimental electronic chalkboards. *(For more information about forming local partnerships, see Chapter 6.)*

If donations are not feasible, explore the possibility of lowering costs for equipment purchases and maintenance contracts by purchasing equipment jointly with other schools. In many cases there is no reason why such arrangements need to be limited to the bounds of a school district. Indeed, as money becomes harder and harder to stretch, it might well be worthwhile for principals, superintendents, and/or school board members to consider jointly bidding on some purchases with other town or city agencies or nearby colleges.

Automation and Resource Sharing

Nowhere has automation been used to better effect than in libraries. In fact, one of the chief reasons for computerizing library catalogs and routine library functions such as the purchase and circulation of materials is to free up staff time for more important activities such as working with teachers and students.

There are two basic routes a school can take when automating its library. One is to establish a stand-alone system, which is self-contained within the school, and the other is to participate in a system that is shared with a number of libraries. To the school or school district committed to resource-based learning, only the latter is a real option. While participating in a consortium and/or simply buying into an automated system that services other libraries may cause some loss of autonomy, this is a small price to pay for the wealth of resources that can be accessed through your school's computer. Suddenly the holdings of nearby public and academic libraries can be accessed as readily as your own school's. In addition, more and more libraries sharing online systems are also jointly purchasing and bringing online other databases ranging from an encyclopedia to local community information. Not only is this wealth of information a boon for students, but teachers also benefit as they plan school projects or pursue their own educational interests.

CARL, which is one such library information system, was developed by the research libraries in Colorado. It is now used by all types of libraries throughout the state and in a number of other states as well. For instance, among the more recent sites to come online with CARL are the elementary, middle, and high school libraries of the Denver Public Schools. This system automates the housekeeping activities of these libraries and also opens up access to the holdings of libraries across the state. Having access to CARL also lets these schools choose among other library networks they may wish to view on their public access catalogs (PACs). Among many other online databases available to Denver school students is indexing to hundreds of thousands of journal articles that are housed in the state's research libraries. If students want an article not owned by their school library, they can simply request it through interlibrary loan; but if principals or teachers need an article in a hurry, they can type in a MasterCard or Visa number, and the article will be faxed to their school or, in some cases, shown on the screen.

If it is not possible for your school to buy into such a system, you still have a couple of other options. For example, without any cost to your school, you still may be able to access a system like CARL because it may be offered to the general public by publicly supported institutions. Another way to make many PACs available to your school is to access them via Internet through a nearby campus or a state created network. In either case, only a computer with a modem is required, and once those out-of-pocket costs are paid, usually the only additional expense is the charge for local telephone calls.

The significant value of such access was underscored by the passage of a bill by the Colorado State Legislature in 1990. This bill authorized funding for the establishment of a "library computing network" called ACCESS Colorado. The first goal of ACCESS Colorado is to ensure that every school—indeed, every citizen—will be able to search the 150 PACs on CARL for the cost of only a local phone call.

If increased access to learning resources is not inducement enough, think how valuable it would be if elementary school students could become users of the same online system that they will use in their future schools, in their public libraries, and in many cases even in the colleges they attend. In Colorado, given the number of libraries on CARL, this reality has become common. Increasingly, students no longer need to be chained to a system that they will never use beyond elementary school.

The main point of this section however is that because of today's information and telecommunications technologies, cooperation with other libraries in your region and in your state can provide enormously expanded resources. Often the efforts at cooperation may be spearheaded by either the state library or a state library organization, but for such efforts to be successful, you may need to get people from the larger community of educators—as well as concerned citizens—to become actively involved in lobbying state legislators to make such opportunities possible. Indeed, any effort you spend exploring such options would be well worth your time because possibilities, such as those just described, would not only enhance a resource-based program at your school but also greatly contribute toward facilitating lifelong learning for all people in your state. *(For other resources available to support resource-based learning efforts in your school, see Chapter 6.)*

ADDITIONAL FUNDING

Even if your library's present resources are being used to their fullest and your staff is taking advantage of all available community options, you may still need or want to increase your library's collections and/or purchase new equipment. There is, of course, no single best way to find additional sources of revenue; however, the first thing that you should look at is how you are using your discretionary funds to support your resource-based learning efforts. Such funds carry a double whammy, for besides actually empowering you to buy more technology, they also offer tangible proof of your personal commitment to resource-based learning. *(This issue is discussed further in Chapter 8.)*

As Principal Dangremond pointed out, you also may want to try a little creative financing. She explained by saying, "Fortunately, if you want to implement a resource-based program, it doesn't take a great deal of money. I was able to draw from my building budget, my instructional supplies budget, and my capital outlay budget." She added, "I tried to put as much money into it as I could." Then she went on to say that she also applied for two city foundation grants that provided some start-up money for innovative projects. She said, "We've been able to purchase some multicultural puppets with one grant, and recently we funded our telecommunication project with the other." In addition, she reported that her school's PTO recently bought the media center a laser disk video. She concluded by saying, "Last but not least, we've had a few private contributions from parents—particularly in the form of books and used computers."

As the benefits of resource-based learning become more evident, you also may find that your priorities are changing. Principal Rhodes certainly found that happening to her. She reported, "My priorities go back to my belief of what learning is all about. However, even though I was setting my priorities differently, there really was no additional cost." She explained, "For example, because our new priority was books, I was able to take all the money that was allocated for workbooks and bought books: reading materials, wonderful literature books, multiple copies of books (fiction, nonfiction), and author studies. This was our emphasis—our priority. As a result, the money was just allocated differently."

The most radical suggestion for realigning expenditures to match priorities, however, came from Principal Harvey.

> I guess one issue that we often tend to avoid is that we put substantial amounts of money into the purchasing of basal reading programs in all our schools

throughout the nation. Until we begin to look at redirecting or reallocating some of that money into materials for the library media center or into the development of materials that would be supportive of thematic units, we're not going to go very far because there are not going to be lots of dollars that can be added to the budget for resource-based learning.

But clearly nationwide, we've spent millions of dollars providing every child with a basal reader, and yet what we really have come to realize is that we don't need to do every story in a basal reader, we don't need to do the stories in the sequence they appear, and we don't need to do every chapter test. When that realization occurs, you then look at the cost of implementing the basal reading program, and you must conclude that clearly here are some dollars that can be reallocated.

Principal Harvey concluded with this question: "How much money would you have to put into learning resources if you quit buying basal readers and perhaps even some textbooks?"

New Sources of Funds. The products of some of your students' projects might be another source of funding. Chris Skrzeczynski, a teacher-librarian at Our Lady of the Rosary Primary School in Kenmore, Queensland, Australia, tells how her school's most successful fund-raiser did not even begin as a money-making venture. She reported the following.

> My first venture was to create a school calendar. I cite this as a particular example because it has become a tradition in our school and does not stand as a fund-raiser alone but as an integral part of the school program.
>
> The calendar is produced by children as part of a particular learning unit that is occurring throughout the school. Below are listed the themes we have pursued to date:
>
> 1984 The Olympic Games
>
> 1985 In and Around Our School

1986 Books We Enjoy
1987 Leisure Time
1988 The Bicentenary
1989 Around the World
1990 Into the Future
1991 Conservation
1992 Dinosaurs
1993 Toyland
1994 Aussie Antics

Every child in the school submits black-and-white drawings based on the annual theme. From these drawings, 14 are selected for presentation in the calendar and others for the front and back covers. We make sure that all grade levels are represented on the calendar. Other children are involved in the presentation of a "telephone number" page and a "term dates" page. Each of these pages is faced with a child's picture—hence the 14 mentioned above: one for each month and two more. Because all of the children sign their names on the "autograph page," everyone is ultimately represented on the calendar. It is easy to see why these calendars are such a successful venture.

While your school may not want to get into the calendar-making business, you may want to pick up on another fund-raising idea that also grew out of the resource-based learning program at Our Lady of the Rosary Primary School. Because family members and friends could not always come to the school when the students presented their final products from integrated theme units, school personnel decided to videotape the presentations. Skrzeczynski said, "The videotapes make wonderful gifts, but they also give the students an opportunity to acquire an informal portfolio of their accomplishments that they can keep throughout their lives." She concluded, "The popularity of this enterprise has been astonishing!"

When Information Specialist Carter (Sands) took a half-time position at a middle school in New Hampshire in 1988, she found that the library's collection consisted of about 2,000 books, mostly discards from the local high school, with an average copyright date of 1965. This situation, however, was better than the one she had encountered a few years earlier at the elementary school, where the approximately 1,000 books had an average copyright date of 1954. Her budget in each school was only $2,000. Was she defeated? She said,

> In both buildings my main goal was finding some additional funding. How would I find funding? How would I get resources? How do you do resource-based learning under those conditions? Well, let me tell you, it can be done! Because I focused on student learning, the money came. It came from businesses, from parents, from adopt-a-book programs, and gradually from the school. Then support began to come from the classroom teachers. Instead of their questioning, "Who is getting the book money?", they began to say, "I would rather see those books put into the library than into the classroom." That was a real turnabout!

Carter (Sands), of course, is an extraordinary person; few library media specialists could have accomplished all that she did under the same circumstances. However, if your library media specialist will follow her or his practice of spending time with teachers after each collaborative learning unit to evaluate what has worked well and what could be improved, teachers' demand for learning resources will continue to increase. Then, with your support, subsequent shifts in resource allocations will happen based on needs identified by teachers rather than because of a top-down mandate based on anticipated needs for an unproven program.

CHAPTER 6
CONNECTING WITH COMMUNITY RESOURCES

> **"**A school library media center really is a programming center—the heartbeat of the school. It's the core of the school...the place where a lot of things happen."
>
> TOM CELIK, SENIOR VICE PRESIDENT OF
> THE HILLS BANK AND TRUST COMPANY, IOWA CITY, IA

THIS CHAPTER IS REALLY AN EXTENSION OF THE previous one because it covers in greater depth the critical issue of forming partnerships in the community in order to ensure the success of resource-based learning at your school. Although all educators are instinctively aware of the importance of partnering in this day and age of tight and/or shrinking budgets, the National Association of Partners in Education, Inc. (NAPE), a member of the National Forum on Information Literacy, is one of a number of organizations that has been established in recent years to document how essential community involvement is to quality education.

The following highlights from NAPE's November 1991 issue of *National School District Partnership Survey* will establish the context for the ensuing discussion on the value of a school's partnership with the community. *(For more information about*

NAPE, write to the National Association of Partners in Education, Inc., 209 Madison Ave., Suite 301, Alexandria, VA 22314.)

- In the 1989–1990 school year, over half—51 percent—of American school districts had active partnership programs.
- Partnership programs involve the impressive total of approximately 2.6 million volunteers.
- The combined value of the goods and services contributed in 1989–1990 by the sponsors of partnership programs was nearly $1 billion.
- The most frequently cited sponsors of partnership programs are parent organizations, confirming the continued vital role parents play in the nation's schools.
- Partnership programs are closely tied to the national goals as shown in the strong emphasis on academic achievement in the content subjects . . . .[p. 3]

The survey also found that the use of volunteers in schools "is a serious response to serious educational problems that face the nation today and for some time to come." It also confirmed "the importance of the contribution made by business and community programs and the substantive nature of their involvement in the educational process." [p. 17]

The following examples of partnering with individuals and organizations, all of which have the potential to support resource-based learning programs, are offered in the hope of giving you some fresh, practical ideas to pursue.

CONNECTING WITH COMMUNITY MEMBERS

The Iowa City Community School District believes that involving community members in the educational process is so important that it created and funded a half-time position of Volunteer Coordinator in 1992. Terry Blevins, who was hired to fill this position, feels that "the possibilities for volunteers are endless."

At the beginning of her newly created position, Blevins asked all of the elementary principals to determine their needs. They unanimously agreed that they needed people to read to children on a one-on-one basis. In response, Blevins organized the Rockin' Readers, a group of volunteer senior citizens who read to children. She asks each Rockin' Reader to commit to at least one hour a week for six weeks, but she reported that some read as many as six hours a week and that no one left the program after the first six weeks. In fact, when some of these volunteers go to Florida for a couple months in the winter, they maintain their contact with the children by writing to them. Blevins added, "Most of the Rockin' Readers feel that they get more out this experience than the children do!"

Following are some other volunteer programs created by Blevins in the Iowa City Community School District.

- **ESL Partners** are community members who work with children who speak English as a second language. These volunteers get some training and are given a handbook of suggested activities and games that they can play with the students.
- **Senior Pen Pals** are house-bound senior citizens who maintain regular correspondence with children. This volunteer program gives students a real-life reason to write letters to and enables them to learn about life in another generation.
- **Math and Science Mentors** are college or graduate students who work one-on-one with students on the high and low ends of the math and science classes. They cover a wide range of activities, including helping students do homework and taking them on field trips to a chemistry lab on the university campus.

Blevins uses several tactics to get volunteers to fill all of these positions. For example, she said, "I offer to speak about the different volunteer programs at any civic or church group that will have me," and many do. She also works closely with the nearby university, the local senior citizens' group, and the town Volunteer Action Center. Blevins also relies on word-of-mouth recommendations. "That's how we get many of our Rockin' Readers," she said. "A volunteer will tell a friend what a wonderful experience it is, and then the friend will volunteer as well."

Blevins believes that all of the volunteers contribute

greatly to the Iowa City schools by providing one-on-one educational experiences for so many students. She also sees how volunteering makes so many community members feel connected to the schools. As an example, she shared the following story about one grandmother volunteer.

> When this lady first moved to Iowa from Brooklyn, she said that she "simply couldn't care less about the local schools." She had no connection to them because all of her grandchildren were in Brooklyn. However, after she signed up to be a Senior Pen Pal, she realized that she was starting to read everything in the newspaper about the schools. Next, she wanted to visit one of the schools, and now she is a permanent volunteer in one of the elementary school libraries. In fact, if we ever have to count on someone to help out, we know we can call on her. She certainly is an excellent example of how volunteer work benefits both sides; the school gets her help, and she has a very rewarding focal point in her life.

At the Lincoln Elementary School in Iowa City, the entire student publishing center is run by parent volunteers. Chris Kolarik, the principal of that school, explained that the publishing center was first created to give students another reason for revising and editing their writing. After she and several teachers studied the process and visited other students' publishing centers, they developed their own.

Key to making the center work was a dependable staff of volunteers. To find such volunteers, Kolarik put notices in the school's newsletters and gave a special presentation about the publishing center at a back-to-school night. "Out of those volunteers," Kolarik said, "I was looking for one strong leader who could run the operation of the center and coordinate the other volunteers." So far, the school has been fortunate to find such a leader as well as anywhere from eight to twelve other volunteers a year. "Now," Kolarik said, "we also get a lot of new volunteers from word-of-mouth from one parent to another."

The Tecumseh-Harrison Elementary School in Vincennes, Indiana, which the April 1993 issue of *Redbook* magazine named as one of most outstanding schools in the United States, has an even more extensive volunteer program. William Hopper, principal of that school, explained that he has never underestimated the desire nor the willingness of the people in the community—especially the parents—to work with the students. He said, "We even go as far as hanging a 'Welcome Parents' sign over the main entrance of the school because we want them here."

Hopper gets many people to volunteer by sending a "Lend-a-Hand" form home with the students at the beginning of the year. On the form *(see Figure 6.1 on page 92)* he solicits both general-needs volunteers and special-talent volunteers. Those who volunteer provide staff support and also contribute to resource-based programs in a second way: They enable students to learn directly from an expert as opposed to learning from secondary sources such as printed materials or a teacher's lecture.

An example of such direct benefits is the Tecumseh-Harrison Elementary School's successful Arts in Education program, in which local and statewide artists are invited to the school to demonstrate their particular expertise. In the 1992–1993 school year, for example, the school had four "artists-in-residence": a papermaker, a printmaker, a storyteller, and a dancer. The school makes a great effort, as well, to integrate these artists into the school curriculum. The papermaker, for instance, worked with the science teacher that year on his unit on the environment and recycling.

Following are examples of some of the other ways that volunteers enhance the educational process at the Tecumseh-Harrison School.

- After some informal training by the teachers, parent volunteers work with students as instructional facilitators and help in the school's publishing center, which publishes as many as 2,000 student books a year.

FIGURE 6.1

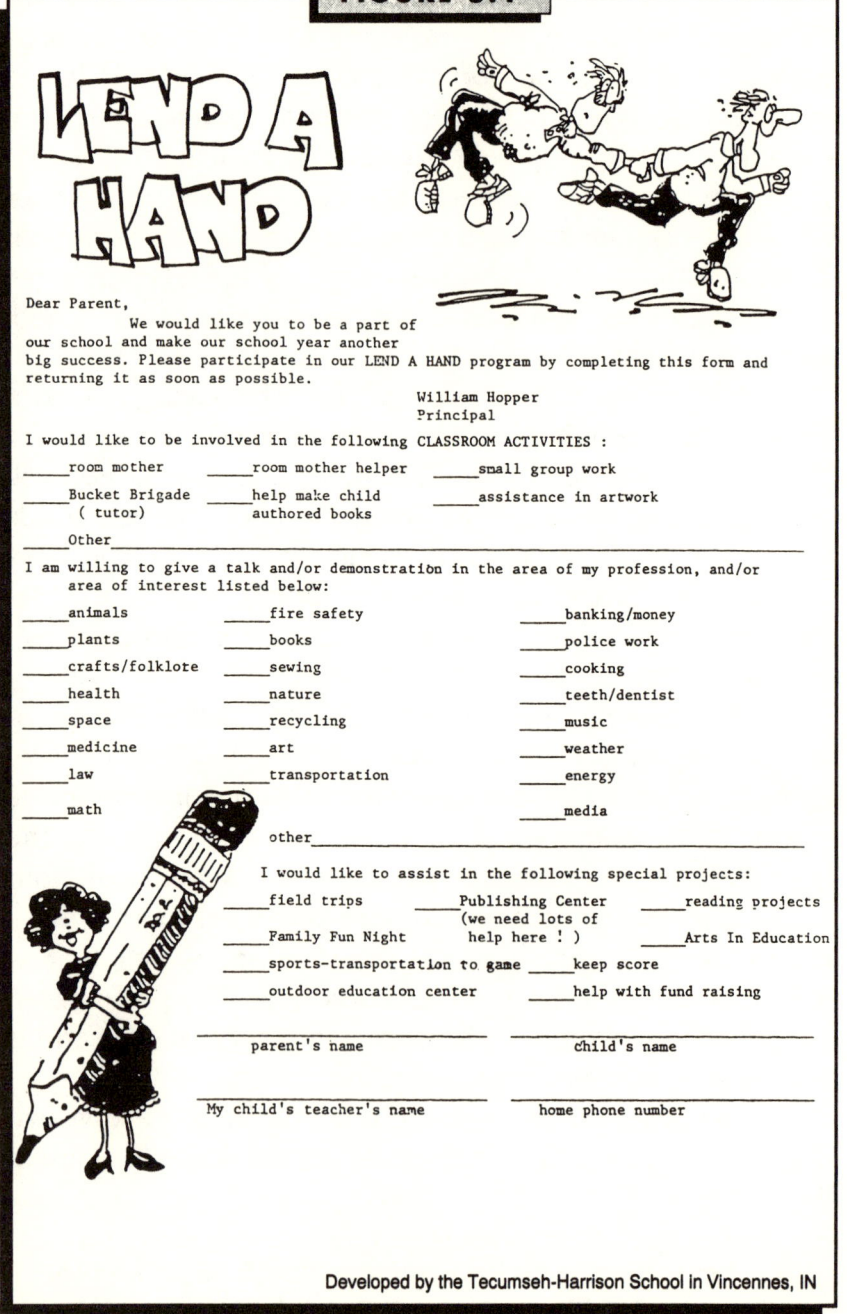

LEND A HAND

Dear Parent,
   We would like you to be a part of our school and make our school year another big success. Please participate in our LEND A HAND program by completing this form and returning it as soon as possible.

                                William Hopper
                                Principal

I would like to be involved in the following CLASSROOM ACTIVITIES :

____room mother   ____room mother helper   ____small group work

____Bucket Brigade ____help make child   ____assistance in artwork
     (tutor)   authored books

____Other_____

I am willing to give a talk and/or demonstration in the area of my profession, and/or area of interest listed below:

____animals	____fire safety	____banking/money
____plants	____books	____police work
____crafts/folklore	____sewing	____cooking
____health	____nature	____teeth/dentist
____space	____recycling	____music
____medicine	____art	____weather
____law	____transportation	____energy
____math		____media

____other_____

I would like to assist in the following special projects:

____field trips   ____Publishing Center   ____reading projects
                        (we need lots of
____Family Fun Night   help here !)   ____Arts In Education

____sports-transportation to game ____keep score

____outdoor education center   ____help with fund raising

_____   _____
   parent's name   child's name

_____   _____
My child's teacher's name   home phone number

Developed by the Tecumseh-Harrison School in Vincennes, IN

- In the school's "Read Me a Story" program, parents volunteer to read stories to individual students or to small groups of students. In the intermediate "Reading Helpers" program, other volunteers work with older students.
- The school also works with the local R.S.V.P. center to bring senior citizens into the school to tutor individual students. Principal Hopper said, "We have found that these senior citizens make significantly longer commitments with each successive school year."
- Even McDonald's sends volunteers. During the downtime at a nearby McDonald's, several employees walk to the school and work with students for half-hour periods.
- Through a program called "Initial Experience," Vincennes University sends over education students to work at the elementary school for one hour three times a week for a semester to tutor students on a one-on-one basis. The students gain some firsthand experience while offering the teachers some much appreciated help.
- Over the years many college professors have also shared with the students their expertise in the areas of science, history, and language arts. Principal Hopper reported that "even Dr. Phillip Summers, the university president, takes time out of his busy schedule to read to our students or to talk to them about the importance of making good grades."

Community members, of course, can volunteer more than just their time. For example, Betty and Craig Watts recently donated $10,000 to the Tecumseh-Harrison Elementary School to fully fund a computer lab for their son's class of 14 mildly mentally handicapped nine-year-olds. "Computers have a magic way of teaching our son Ryan," Mrs. Watts said, "and I wanted him to have what he needs." Commenting on the donation, Principal Hopper said, "Nothing like this has ever happened in all my years in education." Originally, the Watts were going to make their donation anonymously because, as Mrs. Watts pointed out, "We didn't want anyone to think we were tooting our own horns." However, after thinking about it for a while, they changed their minds because they felt that other financially able parents might also help their children's schools if they heard about their donation.

The downside of a volunteer program, of course, is that recruiting, organizing, and training volunteers take time. However, according to educators who have successful volunteer programs, that investment of time is repaid a hundredfold. As a result of individualized help, students' work improves as their self-esteem and self-confidence grow, and, of course, the volunteers themselves benefit by feeling committed to the school. Community members' concerned interest in the schools can only pay off again and again whenever budget issues get put before the community for a vote. There is not the slightest doubt that an extensive volunteer program will greatly enhance the educational opportunities and the successes of a resource-based learning program at your school.

School-Community Projects. In addition to involving community members in volunteer programs, some schools have drawn community members into the actual learning process itself. For example, Library Media Specialist Coatney planned an all-school project on explorers in all fields. After applying for a foundation grant to cover the cost of costumes, she went to a PTO meeting and told the parents, "I want the kids to meet as many wonderful people in history as they can because I think they will begin to see some common patterns. For instance, they will begin to see that it isn't luck that makes people successful; it's hard work." At that meeting, Coatney not only got the support of the organization for the project, but she also got six volunteers to participate in the final program. Next on Coatney's agenda was to ask teachers to volunteer to portray various historical characters. In the end, 19 volunteers agreed to participate.

After the volunteers chose one explorer from a list of 40, they spent part of their summer vacation reading about their character and preparing a 15-minute presentation. Coatney also spent the summer creating activities in all subject areas that would involve the students in projects pertaining to the various explorers. For example, if students chose Columbus as their explorer, some studied math by going outside and measuring off the size of Columbus's ships in meters and feet.

Finally, after six weeks of various student activities and presentations, all of the volunteers gave their presentations. Then the students noted the names of the different explorers on a giant timeline in the gymnasium. "This experience used the combination of students, teachers, and parents in a unique—and valuable—way," Coatney added.

Another exceptional school project that included many community participants occurred in 1992 at the (K–4) North Side School in East Williston, New York. Lillian Krasner and Jeanne Bouza-Rose, resource room teachers at North Side; and Glenn Pribek, the district's social studies coordinator, planned a huge celebration for the school's 75th anniversary. During the preceding year, the teachers had formed a research team of 20 fourth graders who worked throughout the year to produce a 30-page booklet that explored the school's beginnings. In the preface, fourth graders Phillip Fort, Matthew Singleton, and Adam Cohen wrote the following account of their research efforts.

> Being a researcher is like being a detective. Digging up information, going around to find the history of North Side School, that's what we've been doing for the past months. You can't imagine how we've worked for our school's anniversary, but we enjoyed it. We met together in school and out of school, we got people to help by giving us information and pictures, we interviewed former students and members of the community, and we took trips to the library.
>
> Twenty fourth graders took part in researching the world, the community, and North Side School in 1917. We gathered information and once we had it, each student decided what topic he or she would enjoy working on.

Some researchers on the "World" committee wrote to corporations such as Crayola, Mercedes Benz, Whitman's Chocolates, and Planters Peanuts because they were in business at the time our school was built. They asked for information about their products now and in 1917 so they could make comparisons.

Mr. Pribek made plans for us to go to Wheatley High School to get more information. Once we got to the library, Mr. Singer, the librarian, showed us the microfilm machine. Everybody crowded around it to see the pictures of a 1917 issue of the *New York Times*. There were advertisements from Macy's and Lord and Taylor. A man's suit was $9.00! When we were done, Mr. Singer gave us books about transportation, entertainment, fashion, and technology for us to look through. It was noisy, but it was excited noisy.

The Town Hall is on Plandome Road in Manhasset. Mrs. Banks is the Town Clerk. We met Mrs. Rose and Mrs. Krasner there during the spring vacation. While we were there, the town photographer...gave us photographs showing what our area looked like at the beginning of the 20th century. The Town Hall keeps records of every town meeting that has ever taken place, back to the 1700s....

This will give you some idea of what we did as we worked together researching. When we began investigating, there was so much we didn't know. As we got organized and sorted out information, we found out a lot about our past. We hope you will gain an interest in history from this book, which we dedicate to North Side School on its 75th birthday.

Other entries in the booklet that reflected what students had learned about history were entitled "The World at War," "Woman Suffrage," and "President Woodrow Wilson." Another page included a timeline compiled by two fourth graders that showed all of the town's major events between 1917 and 1992. The students also included entries in areas such as fashion, transportation, and technology—past and present. They even reprinted a page from the 1916 ledger of the Griffin General Store and one from the 1918 school register that included a note about an influenza epidemic. One student reported on the fire that destroyed the first building on the grounds, and the booklet ended with memories of former students.

The week-long final celebration of the school's 75th birthday began with the ringing of church bells all over the city. Other events were a 1917 dress-up day, a lawn picnic, and a huge birthday cake. Another important event was the performance of the play *Time Warp,* which was written by approximately 20 third graders. Following is the introduction to that play.

> The play you are about to see was the idea of a group of third graders. They wanted to entertain you and teach you at the same time. All the facts in our play are true. They are based on information given to us by Mrs. Norma Seaman, a lady who was born in East Williston in 1913. The names of the characters in the play are the names of real children who attended North Side in 1917. So sit back and let your imagination take over. We hope you enjoy our play, *Time Warp.*

This project spanned a whole year and involved most community members in one way or another. Although planning and executing this event was an immense job, its value to the fourth graders who did the research and to all the other school and community participants was equally immense. It was a real-life experience that taught them lifelong skills and showed them the value of cooperation. *(For more information about this project, write to the Board of Cooperative Educational Services of Nassau County, 234 Glen Cove Road, Carle Place, NY 11514.)*

CONNECTING WITH PUBLIC LIBRARIES

The preceding chapter urged you and your library media specialist to assess your present collections and equipment before purchasing anything new. A part of that assessment should always take into consideration the resources available to your school through your local public library.

Schools that have embraced resource-based learning have found ways to build on long-established traditions like visits to the public library by considering what new affiliations they can establish. For example, rather than just taking the children in your school for a yearly visit to the public library to get library cards, consider what arrangements could be made to give them access to any or all of the library's services and resources. How can its summer reading program be tied into your end-of-school activities; or, if the library offers no summer reading program, how can school personnel work with library staff to create and support one?

Another connection you should consider is displaying students' products from learning projects in the public library or some other public building. Perhaps such a display could be the basis of a program that would encourage parents to go to the library with their children and learn about materials and services that would be of personal interest to them as parents and as working adults. Perhaps your school could send home notices of events at the public library that would be of interest to family members.

Considering the documented relationship between academic success and parental involvement, anything you do to promote parents' use of public libraries would certainly enhance student performance. For instance, the following findings from *Reading In and Out of School,* which was first mentioned in Chapter 3, stress the importance of family influence in developing lifelong readers.

- The amount of reading that students do out of school is positively related to their reading achievement. Yet, students report relatively little reading out of school.
- At all three grades [4, 8, and 12], students who reported more reading materials in the home had higher average reading achievement . . . [but] students reported somewhat less access to reading materials in the home in 1990 than in 1988.

- Eighth and twelfth graders who lived with adults who read frequently had higher average reading achievement. However, less than one-half reported that the adults in their home read "a lot."
- At all three grades, students who reported talking about their readings with their friends and families on at least a monthly basis had higher average reading achievement. About one fourth of the students reported never having such discussions or doing so only yearly.
- Students who reported watching more television had lower average reading achievement. In 1990, 62 percent of the fourth graders reported watching three or more hours of television each day (25 percent of these watched six hours or more). [pp. 5–6]

The report concluded that "students who reported more home support for literacy had higher average reading achievement."

No one in public education would deny that young people's acquiring the habit of using public libraries will stand them in good stead for the rest of their lives. Nevertheless, efforts at cooperation between school and public libraries have been only partly successful in the past. Although there has been much discussion about combining services over the years, little has come of it. Unfortunately, far too often there has been friction between public libraries and schools because teachers usually give assignments that will be pursued largely at public libraries without consulting with librarians in advance.

Nevertheless, there are two compelling reasons why close coordination between school library media centers and public libraries is essential. First, since the main purpose of resource-based learning is to prepare students for lifelong learning, it is crucial that students regularly have positive research experiences in public libraries. Students also need to learn at an early age that no one information source and/or library contains all the information they need. Second, as the previous chapter pointed out, budget constraints coupled with the need for a rich base of learning materials dictate cooperative collection building.

Helena Zobec, writing in the August 1990 issue of *Access,* the major Australian journal for public and school librarians, stressed this second point by saying that in the near future cooperation is going to be essential. She wrote, "School and public libraries are going to have to deal with the reality of change. Not only will resources have to be shared in the future, but so will staff and programs." She went on to say, "The lines of communication between school and public libraries need to be opened." She suggested, for example, that teachers supply public librarians with information about school assignments and that they familiarize themselves with all of the resources of the public library and encourage their students to use them.

Here in the United States, some cooperation is already taking place, although it is surprising how few schools are in contact with nearby public libraries. There are, of course, some exceptions. In San Antonio, for example, two elementary schools donated land on the corners of their playgrounds for a branch of the public library. As a result, Director Dobrot reported that "there's lots of traffic between those schools and the public libraries, which is a real great advantage for those kids and their teachers."

In some areas where resource-based learning is not in place and schools have little interest in working with the public libraries, public librarians have taken it upon themselves to initiate the connection. This certainly was the case with Marian Lattanzio, the head of Children's Services at the Lucy Robbins Wells Library in Newington, Connecticut. As you read the following account of this public librarian who has a deep and abiding concern for the children in her community, keep in mind that you could suggest each of her initiatives to your own public librarian.

Lattanzio's first initiative was to call on the school

principals. Echoing what the school library media specialists had emphasized in the interviews for this book, Lattanzio said, "Without their support, I couldn't get anything going." She cautioned other public librarians, however, by stressing the need for "some assertiveness and a lot of perseverance" because forming a partnership with public libraries does not seem to come naturally to either principals or school library media specialists in most traditional settings.

Eventually, Lattanzio was able to get the principals into friendly competition with the public library's summer reading program. As a result, she was invited to a couple of the principals' meetings, where she helped work out creative strategies for cooperating more closely with the schools. For example, one result of such a meeting was the formulation of a letter to families new in town. The letter encouraged the parents to bring their children to the public library to get library cards, because having access to the resources in the public library would help their children with their studies. Lattanzio added, "One of the nicest outcomes from my working with the principals is their participation in the National Library Week. Because the public schools are closed that week for spring vacation, the principals have the opportunity to come into the library and read to the children. They love it and the kids love it."

Lattanzio's perseverance has paid off in other ways as well. The principals now invite her to a teachers' meeting at the beginning of each year, and she is able to reinforce how the public library can help the students with their assignments. Perhaps most importantly, the principals are now also giving release time to their own library media specialists to plan cooperative activities with Lattanzio. As a result of these meetings, Lattanzio and the school library media specialists have been able to eliminate unnecessary duplication of resources, such as magazine subscriptions. Lattanzio now also sends out

Educator's Newsletter that includes an "Assignment Alert" form, which teachers now automatically fill out and send in before their students go to the library to research a special project.

When the schools' budgets were cut a while ago, Lattanzio also started a resource center at the library. There teachers can find many monthly publications such as *Instructor* magazine, which had been eliminated from the schools' purchases, and reading activity guides that supplement trade books. In addition, Lattanzio holds in-service workshops to show teachers how to use any new technology, such as the library's on-line public access catalog.

Through the principals, Lattanzio also makes sure she reaches the students at crucial stages of their development. For example, every year she invites all sixth graders and their teachers for a tour of the library. She and other staff members point out various areas—such as the young adult paperback section, the reference section, and various resources in the children's room like the online public access catalog. With a little surprise in her voice, Lattanzio said, "In many cases, the teachers are more impressed than the students by all that they see!" She explained that, for example, many teachers had no idea that the reference section in the children's room contained *Science Experiments on File* by Facts on File—an essential book for any school that is going to hold a science fair.

"What comes out of all of this sharing is that I now have a firmer grasp of the schools' curriculum," Lattanzio concluded. "As a result, I've been able to develop the collection to support the curriculum in the past five years." In spite of the many connections that Lattanzio has been able to make with the schools, she plans to make even more. For example, sometime in the future she would like the public library to be on-line with all of the schools.

Lattanzio's message for principals is to do whatever you can to encourage active partnering between your library media specialist and personnel from your local public library. Everyone will benefit—especially the students.

CONNECTING WITH BUSINESSES

Chapter 5 recommended that before you buy any equipment, you should find out what contributions of new or used equipment local businesses will give you. Although you probably will not be able to get all the equipment you want or need through donations, any gifts can add to the quality of education at your school. For example, to help disadvantaged, learning disabled, and home-bound students at the Darnestown Elementary School in Gaithersburg, Maryland, Radio Shack donated ten laptop computers with internal modems. The school uses them in two ways: for home-to-school computer use through modem links for searching databases on CD-ROM units at the school, and for school use in a small computer lab and in the classroom for modem link to the IMC for searches. The school believes that these donated computers will help the students (1) gain the computer skills they will need in the future; (2) improve their self-image and build their self-confidence and leadership capabilities; and (3) open their world by teaching them how to use telecommunications and computers. In an announcement the school said, "Realizing the fact that current first grade students at our school will graduate from high school in the year 2000, we are attempting to direct our instructional focus on educating children for the 21st century." The likelihood of reaching this goal improved with the donation of the laptop computers.

Sometimes local companies will donate the money to buy equipment rather than the equipment itself. For example, Dr. Violet Harada, head of School Library Services in Honolulu, Hawaii, wrote,

"For the past year, our office has been working with two elementary school libraries in Hawaii that are using CD-ROM technology as an integral part of their school program. The purchase of hardware and software was made possible through a special Chevron grant as part of a school library/business partnership."

In the grant proposal to Chevron, Dr. Harada listed the following project objectives:

- To engage students in creative learning opportunities that integrate database searching as a way to find information and as a way to build understanding of concepts in various disciplines.
- To enable students to develop critical thinking skills in formulating simple search strategies.
- To involve students in cooperative problem-solving assignments.
- To encourage students in exploring resourceful ways to use and communicate their findings.

This school district has the opportunity of reaching these goals because it not only saw the value of partnering with a local business, but it also put in the effort necessary to make it happen.

Another way schools can benefit from a partnership with business is to arrange to use and test equipment to make sure it meets their needs before committing to it. This is the approach that the Grand Haven Area Public Schools in Michigan took with IBM when they wanted technological help in restructuring their schools' curricular approach. According to district technology coordinator Carol Breen, IBM agreed to help the Peach Plains Elementary School staff integrate technology into the daily instructional process.

The first phase of the plan involved the networking of 9 classrooms and 45 computers with the media center. IBM not only supplied the necessary software for a one-year pilot program in grades 4, 5, and 6, but it also provided staff training. In explaining the restructuring program to the local Board of Education, Melinda Edison, principal of Peach Plains, said, "We envision the belief that ALL children can learn will replace previous assumptions that some kids can't." Here is a school district that sees students as individuals rather than as robots programmed to do only certain tasks. What's more, partnerships with businesses can greatly enhance a school's ability to meet students' individual needs.

The list of examples could go on and on, but getting such support from businesses, of course, does not just happen. For many people, asking for help and not becoming overly discouraged by some rejections are the hardest parts of the job. You must always remember that large companies are constantly being asked for help by people representing many very worthwhile concerns. On the other hand, the old cliché is true: nothing ventured, nothing gained.

As you lay the groundwork for your request, consider three actions that will give your school an edge over your competitors. First, whenever possible document that children of the company's employees and/or customers attend your school. Second, detail how the resources/equipment you are requesting will fit into a well thought out plan that will guarantee their effective use in helping students learn. It is only common sense that companies will take more seriously any proposal that promises that their donated equipment will be integrated into the actual learning process—rather than be merely an add-on to the curriculum. Third, in any proposal, specify "what's in it" for the company. For example, instruction at Clearspring Elementary School is definitely being enhanced by using GTE's electronic chalkboard at the same time that GTE is getting some valuable feedback from the school about how the new equipment could actually be used.

Partnerships beyond Equipment. In Holland, Michigan, every elementary, middle, and high school has formed a partnership with a local business, but as Principal Dangremond explained, this is a different kind of partnership—a closer and more intimate one. Her school, for example, formed a partnership with the First Michigan Bank, which is located directly across the street. The mission statement for that partnership reads as follows.

> To foster a partnership between Lakeview School and First Michigan Bank to strengthen the educational process and to develop a positive sense of community by giving students the opportunity to practice life skills related to banking and personal skills essential for success and to enrich the classroom curriculum through the study of money, workplace values, problem solving, and technology.

When establishing this partnership, Dangremond worked closely with Deb Sterkin, the partnership coordinator, a position funded by the Holland Education Foundation. "It was important to us," Dangremond said, "that the partnership went both ways. We didn't want the partner to do all the giving; we wanted to be able to give back to the partner as well."

After giving all of the Lakeview students a tour of the bank—taking them inside the vaults, and showing them how the ATM machine works—bank officials helped set up a student branch of the bank in a hallway at the school. After fifth graders filled out applications for positions as bank manager, tellers, and supply clerks, they were interviewed by bank officials, Principal Dangremond, and a teacher. Then they were "hired" to run the bank, which was named—through a school contest—Michigan's Smallest Bank.

Before the bank actually opened, the students took home forms to get parents' permission to open accounts, and in conjunction with the study of mathematics, teachers explained how a bank works. On the day of the Grand

Opening, the bank manager took the student manager out to lunch to discuss the responsibilities of the position. Then at the official opening ceremonies at the school, both bank managers gave a short speech, and together they cut a red ribbon.

Since then, the school and the bank have held many joint activities. The bank employees helped the students with their canned food drive, and the students have invited the bank employees to a breakfast. In fact, the students write letters to bank employees inviting them to all the school functions. "We've done as much as we possibly can to involve the bank employees in education in as many ways as possible," Dangremond explained, "because people who do not have school-aged children often don't have any contact with the schools. Once they do, of course, they're thrilled to see the teaching process and get involved in it." In return, the students are learning lifelong skills that are both essential and very exciting.

Library Media Coordinator van Deusen described a partnership with another bank, the Hills Bank and Trust Company in Iowa City. This partnership, however, extends beyond the school into the community. Since 1988, the local schools, the public libraries, and the bank have sponsored a Community Reading Month. Following are the goals of this unique partnership.

- To encourage everyone in Iowa City and the Coralville area to read.
- To provide children and parents enriching experiences related to reading.
- To recognize the significant contribution of educators.
- To provide an opportunity for the community, the schools, the public libraries, and local businesses to jointly emphasize the value of lifelong learning.
- To provide a community service.

To meet these goals each year, bank officials and school personnel form a committee to plan, organize, and publicize the various events. Committee members from the schools, for instance, decide on the activities, invite appropriate speakers, give book talks, develop curricular activities for teaching literature units based on featured guests, and develop recommended reading lists for children and their parents. The bank officials, on the other hand, provide the funding for the activities, pay for any advertising, contact local businesses and political leaders for endorsement and support, and hold receptions honoring teachers and featured guests. In recent years the monthly activities have included the following.

- **A 15-minute Communitywide Read-in.** Students at all schools, including the local university, read; local radio stations feature readers on the air; and everyone in the community is encouraged to stop whatever they are doing and read for 15 minutes.
- **Book Talks.** School library media specialists and local public librarians cooperate in providing a series of book talks, which are held in the different public libraries. The bank provides a free lunch to anyone who attends.
- **Visiting Author.** Each year the bank pays for a nationally recognized author to spend a week in Iowa City to visit the children in the schools. In 1992, for example, children's book author Janice Lee Smith, who wrote *The Monster in the Third Dresser Drawer,* talked to all of the children in the elementary schools.
- **Reception.** At the end of the month, the bank holds a reception for 300 guests, including teachers, community leaders, and the year's visiting author.

Tom Celik, a senior vice president at the Hills Bank and Trust Company, might seem an unlikely instigator of such activities because as a school board member about ten years before, he had suggested that all of the school libraries might be closed in order to save money. In an interview, he explained this action by saying, "At the time the board was facing some pretty serious budget cuts, and I thought that since I grew up without any libraries and I survived, perhaps this was an area we should consider." He went on to say that after meeting Jean van

Deusen and after his wife became a school teacher, he changed his mind. "A school library media center really is a programming center—the heartbeat of the school," he said. "It's the core of the school . . . the place where a lot of things happen."

The Community Reading Month actually came about somewhat inadvertently. In 1987 the University of Iowa asked the Hills Bank and Trust to sponsor a reception at the university library. Celik said, "I chose the reception in the fall involving children's literature on the theory that it was nine months away, and I liked kids. Then I called Jean, and the reading project came out of the brainstorming for that reception."

Celik went on to explain that from a marketing standpoint, the reading project also benefitted the bank by identifying it as a local community bank. He said, "Since we had a young staff with lots of energy and lots of young kids, reading sort of tied all of this together . . . Reading helps kids, helps adults, and ties families together."

The Hills Bank and Trust also sponsors the Coralville Summer Reading Project. An elementary school principal in Coralville originally suggested this idea to Celik because he felt that the children were not reading very much in the summer. The program begins with a kick-off party at the bank at the beginning of each summer vacation. At that time the children sign up to complete 10 activities out of a group of 20 that relate to reading. The program, which is run on the honor system, ends before school starts in the fall. At that time all the students who have achieved their goals are rewarded with a T-shirt. In the first year of the program only a couple of hundred students participated, but in recent summers over a thousand have joined in. "When you stop to think about it," Celik said, "we've got about a thousand kids running around Coralville wearing our T-shirts. From a marketing standpoint, it is a wonderful event!"

He went on to say, "Personally, I think banks and

businesses make a big mistake by spending too much money on direct advertising. I think buying an ad in the paper is okay, but I think it's better to spend the money on programs like this!" In a serious tone, Celik stressed, "On the other hand, nobody should go into this type of project unless they really believe in it. This is the single most important thing, because if you don't believe in it, it won't work." Then he added, "Everything we do here works because we believe it is the right thing to do, and we have made a personal commitment to it. When we started, we hoped it would have some marketing value, but it was not a requirement. You can't go into a reading project like this saying, 'If we don't bring in 15 new customers, we won't do it'." Pausing for a moment, he concluded, "As a result, I sincerely believe that we have impacted reading in this community. I think the reading project has made a difference; it has made a difference in the kids, in the parents, and even in our staff. It has changed everything."

Summing up the value of these activities from her point of view, Library Media Coordinator van Deusen said, "The whole idea of the Community Reading Month is to focus attention on reading as a lifelong activity and as a skill everyone needs to be a lifelong learner." She added, "And this partnership with the bank is an excellent example of what happens when all kinds of people from different interests collaborate and celebrate together."

OTHER CONNECTIONS

Besides the community resources already described, there are other free or inexpensive resources that can help your school support a resource-based learning program. For example, this book has already touched upon a number of resources that may be available through nearby colleges or universities—such as faculty members and on-line catalogs. In addition, with the great concern for K–12 reform that began in the 1980s, higher education has begun to seriously consider what it can do—besides teacher education—to assist the K–12 sector.

The most substantive result of that expressed concern is the College/School Collaboration Program of the American Association for Higher Education (AAHE), which since 1989 has held an annual conference on what higher education can do to help the K–12 sector. AAHE also features programs on this topic at its annual conventions and publishes related materials. The AAHE resources can be a continuing source of ideas for collaboration between your school and colleges in the area. *(For more information on the AAHE college/school collaboration program, contact AAHE, 1 Dupont Circle, Suite 360, Washington, DC 20036.)* Suggestions for other collaborative activities can be found through ERIC and other educational databases.

Internet Access. One university resource that is literally making the whole planet available to schools is Internet. This extensive international interconnection of computer networks provides online access to hundreds of library catalogs and other information databases—as well as to individuals and to discussion groups on almost any imaginable topic. Until quite recently this network was restricted to higher eduction and research personnel; however, more and more public schools and libraries have been gaining access to it. A PC and modem are the only equipment necessary, but arrangements will have to be made for a hookup to the network. Usually this is done through a nearby college or university. Increasingly, however, state networks of school and/or public libraries are also organizing to provide in-state (and broader) networking through Internet. The cost should be quite minimal; often only the price of a local phone call.

Increasingly, commercial on-line computer networks that provide access to many databases, E-mail, and conference bulletin boards are also becoming available. Some networks, such as ATLIS, are specifically geared toward educational leaders, but others, such as America Online that provides access to Internet, and Prodigy lend themselves to both home and school use. If for some reason you cannot make a connection with Internet, you definitely should explore some of these commercial alternatives.

Through Internet and other on-line systems, students can also communicate with each other through electronic mail. It is impossible to adequately describe the benefit and just plain fun students get through such "correspondence" with other students all over the world, and once a school sees this benefit, it usually encourages its students to use the technology for this purpose. For example, in the January 6, 1993, issue of *The Bobcat Bulletin,* which is published in eastern Maryland, the following cases were reported.

- Students in the first, second, third, and fourth grades sent messages to each other on topics ranging from Halloween to the upcoming elections.
- A 50-state scramble occurred in which a number of classes tried to send and receive E-mail with students in every state. The students proudly displayed wall maps that sprouted flags at each city where successful contact was made.
- A sixth-grade class got involved in a "real-time chat" with students from Connecticut and Denmark on the topic "Global Networking for Youth."
- Students learned the metric system as a result of a message from a student in Denmark who reported that she was 1.59 meters tall and weighed 39 kilos.
- A fifth grader communicated with an electrical engineer in Guatemala.
- Six-, seven-, and eight-year-olds from Iceland, Tasmania, Peru, England, Hawaii, and Maryland participated in KIDNET, an electronic classroom that covered a unit entitled "Houses and Homes."

Television. Starting in 1990, Whittle Communications offered schools a satellite disk, two VCRs, a television set for each classroom, and the cable to hook everything up. In exchange, the schools had to agree to show Whittle's Channel One's twelve minutes of feature stories and news and two minutes of commercials to most students on at least 90 percent of the days school was in session. Some community and school leaders originally objected to their students watching commercials in school; however, the company did get credit for offering news broadcasting and other educational programming geared to students.

Channel One, of course, is not the only television news service aimed specifically at students. *CNN Newsroom,* a noncommercial school news program available since 1989, now reaches 25,000 schools—almost twice the number that subscribe to Channel One. Although Public Television varies from state to state, it also does offer many high-quality programs for students of all ages.

Newspapers. Newspapers are another source of extensive information. Besides being widely available and inexpensive, newspapers in the classroom help build lifelong habits of newspaper reading as well as ensure better informed citizens for tomorrow. In many schools, using newspapers for learning can be enhanced by participating in the Newspapers in Education (NIE) program. Across North America, over 700 newspapers offer NIE and/or newspaper literacy programs that provide curriculum guides to schools—plus significant discounts for classroom subscriptions. Topics of curriculum guides offered by the *Baltimore Sun,* for example, include the following.
- **Newspaper Fun with Garfield (K–3).** Created for the youngest readers, this tabloid contains short, entertaining activities that build skills in language arts, math, and social studies.
- **Taking the Lead (3–6).** This language arts tabloid uses real news stories and advertisements to teach fact finding, creative writing, and other language skills.
- **Body Lessons (4–12).** This tabloid, full of interesting graphics, gives information on health, science, and biology.

- **Historic Pages (4–12).** These pages take students on a trip through time and introduce them to the great events that have helped shape today's world.
- **Prescription for Environmental Health (6–12).** Teachers can promote environmental awareness with this tabloid by getting their students involved in the preservation of the world they are going to inherit.
- **A World of Uniqueness (5–8).** This tabloid helps reduce prejudice by celebrating ethnic diversity and encouraging multicultural understanding.

In addition, publishers involved in NIE programs offer other benefits, such as teacher workshops on how to use newspapers for learning, classroom visits from journalists, and tours of newspaper facilities. *(To find out if there is an NIE program in your area, contact your local newspaper or the Association of American Foundations, the Newspaper Center, 11600 Sunrise Valley Drive, Reston, VA 22091.)*

An on-line service related to newspapers is the nonprofit Youth News Service (YNS). YNS uses computer telecommunications to form a sort of Associated Press for school newspapers. Headquartered in the nation's capital, it shares stories, statistics, and sources with 20 members' bureaus in the United States and Canada. The setup—using computers, phone modems, and electronic mail—is not complicated and is relatively inexpensive. In addition, *YNS News,* a hard-copy version, comes out every two weeks. *(For more information, write to YNS, 2025 Pennsylvania Ave., Washington, DC 20006.)*

Obviously, the resources described in this chapter are just the tip of the iceberg. This small list, however, does make it clear that your school does not have to spend a great deal of money to give students access to rich sources of information far beyond the walls of your building. Once your students have the opportunity to use resources such as the ones described in this chapter, they will benefit not only now but also in the future as they begin to acquire the skills of lifelong learners.

CHAPTER 7
ASSESSMENT OF RESOURCE-BASED LEARNING

> **"**Of all the expenditures that influence a school's effectiveness... the levels of expenditures for library and media services have the highest correlation with student achievement."
>
> WILLIAM BAINBRIDGE, CEO OF SCHOOLMATCH

NOW AS NEVER BEFORE, BOTH PARENTS AND government officials are concerned with measuring educational outcomes, and students merely parroting information on tests is no longer acceptable. Business leaders also have been expressing their concerns about so many students attempting to enter the workforce while lacking the most basic skills. As a result, the National Education Goals continue to be a rallying cry for politicians and even educators who have expressed reservations about the goals but who cannot escape the growing pressure for accountability.

Accountability at the elementary school level, of course, usually means student performance on standardized tests.

Therefore, as a pragmatic school leader, you certainly must ask, "Will resource-based learning help improve overall student performance on standardized tests?" The answer is an unequivocal and resounding *YES!*

INDEPENDENT ASSESSMENT

The most recent in-depth examination of the correlation between resource-based learning and student achievement is a 1992 study by the Colorado Department of Education, which was referred to in Chapter 4. Following are some additional findings of that report.

> This study was undertaken to answer three questions about the relationship between library media programs and academic achievement. Following are those questions and the answers based on the findings of this research:
>
> - Is there, in fact, a relationship between expenditures on LMCs (Library Media Centers) and test performance, particularly when social and economic differences between communities and schools are controlled? Yes. Students at schools with better funded LMCs tend to achieve higher average test scores, whether their schools and communities are rich or poor and whether adults in the community are well or poorly educated.
> - Assuming that there is a relationship between LMC expenditures and test performance, which intervening characteristics of library media programs help to explain this relationship? The size of an LMC's total staff and the size and variety of its collection are important characteristics of library media programs that intervene between LMC expenditures and test performance. Funding is important; but, two of its specific purposes are to ensure adequate levels of staffing in relation to the school's enrollment and a local collection that offers students a large number of materials in a variety of formats.

- Does the performance of an instructional role by library media specialists help to predict test performance? Yes. Students whose library media specialists played such a role—either by identifying materials to be used with teacher-planned instructional units or by collaborating with teachers in planning instructional units—tend to achieve higher average test scores. [p. 97]

The following specific—and somewhat startling—results described in the report should be of great interest to anyone who is considering moving toward a resource-based approach to learning.
- The size of a library media center's staff and collection is the best school predictor of academic achievement. Students who score higher on norm-referenced tests tend to come from schools that have more library media staff and more books, periodicals, and videos.
- Students who score higher on norm-referenced tests tend to come from schools where the instructional role [of the library media specialist] is more prominent.
- Library media expenditures affect LMC staff and collection size and, in turn, academic achievement. Not surprisingly, the size of the LMC collection is related to the amount of funding available for such purposes. Students who score higher on norm-referenced tests tend to come from schools that spend more on library media programs. [p. 96].

While this study does not address resource-based learning per se, all of the conclusions clearly point to the value of that approach. Moreover, Colorado is one of the few states in which there has been strong leadership (including staff development programs) from the Department of Education promoting resource-based learning. The study also serves to highlight research done in this area over the past 30 years. Although the studies are limited in scope, the consistency of the results in terms of the positive impact of library media centers and library media specialists on academic achievement is impressive. *(Research highlights from "The Impact of School Library Media Centers on Academic Achievement" are reprinted in Appendix G on page 185.)*

Another significant and independent source of verification for resource-based learning comes from data collected by SchoolMatch, an information and counseling firm. Located in Columbus, Ohio, this company evaluates schools using its database of comparative information on all 15,892 public school systems and over 12,000 accredited private schools throughout the United States.

In the mid-1980s, SchoolMatch CEO William L. Bainbridge,[1] a former school superintendent, made an important discovery. In response to a request from Bob Edwards, host of National Public Radio's "Morning Edition," Bainbridge told the radio audience on July 13, 1987, about a startling correlation between various school expenditures and student performance on standardized tests. He said, "Of all expenditures that influence a school's effectiveness—including those for families, teachers, guidance services and others—the levels of expenditures for library and media services have the highest correlation with student achievement."

The SchoolMatch results were later published and expanded upon in the June 1988 issue of *American Libraries*. Although no further SchoolMatch studies have been published in this area, Bainbridge recently told us that the correlation between student performance on national scholarship exams and library and media spending levels has continued.

Superintendents also speak about the positive effects of a resource-based approach to learning. James C. Thompson,[2] for example, is always eager to tell about going to the Blue Valley School District in Overland Park, Kansas, as superintendent of schools in 1976. At that time, the district's overall achievement level on the Iowa Basic Skills Test fell between

---

1. Dr. Bainbridge subsequently served on the ALA Presidential Committee on Information Literacy.
2. On January 1, 1993, James Thompson became Superintendent of Schools for the Grapevine-Colleyville Independent School District in Grapevine, TX.

the 60–70 percentiles. By the 1980–1981 school year, the achievement level had risen into the 90 percentile. On many occasions Thompson has said publicly, "Although I cannot verify that the improvement was due to the district's move to resource-based learning, that was the only substantive program change that we had made in the district during that period of time, and I do have the scores to prove that something happened!"

Other schools involved in resource-based learning are just beginning to collect data on changes in student performance. For example, as this book was being written, the R. B. Fernandez Elementary School in San Antonio, was in the process of evaluating changes in student writing scores. Initial reports showed a 14 percent increase in the writing scores of fifth graders over the three-year period since the school had implemented a resource-based approach to learning.

Special Acknowledgements. Documentation of the success of resource-based learning programs comes in other forms as well. For example, sometimes it comes in the form of public recognition as a part of national awards programs. For example, the Oakhill Elementary School in Overland Park, Kansas, won the Presidential Blue Ribbon award during the 1991–1992 school year.

Sharon Coatney, the media specialist at the Oakhill Elementary School, reported that "when our school applied for the award, we presented the library media center as one of the school's strengths—along with the school's history program and its parental involvement." She went on to explain how school personnel had documented the library media center as both the literal and the philosophical center of the school. As such, the library media center influences curriculum planning as well as the school's whole approach to learning.

As a part of the screening process for this award, an evaluator, on contract to the U.S. Department of Education, visited the school. He was the principal of an elementary school that had previously won the award. Coatney said that he didn't seem to understand the library program. "In fact," she said, "he went around the school for two days—just trying to get someone to explain—so that he could understand—what we were doing and how the library really provided the curriculum direction for the entire school."

In another case, Information Specialist Carter (Sands), submitted testimony to the U.S. Senate Labor and Human Resources Committee about her vision of the new school of *America 2000.* Following is the conclusion of her remarks to the committee.

> Change is no longer a choice for our schools. Restructuring, it has been said, is not a spectator sport. Rather we must all work to affect major attitude adjustments throughout our social structure if we are to significantly affect the education of the students who will support us in our retirement and who will provide leadership in an environment where the only constant is change, where information doubles every eighteen months, and where our foremost need is for a generation of "information workers," problem solvers, and decision makers who are consciously participating citizens.

State and national recognition—like these examples—further document the value of a resource-based approach to learning and, in particular, its value to national goals for curriculum reform as projected in the National Education Goals and *America 2000.*

Finally, it is worth noting that resource-based learning is increasingly becoming the centerpiece of educational restructuring. For example, in 1991 Carter (Sands), became a member of a five-person team, whose mission was to prepare for the opening of a "world-class" high school in New Hampshire. Commenting on this opportunity, she said, "The new school of *America 2000* will take the potential of this world-class high school to a vision of society that has not only restructured its educational system but which is also making strides toward meeting the larger social goals of the *America 2000* strategy as well." She went on to explain that at the heart of the new school will be a resource-based learning approach to the curriculum wherein "print, nonprint, human, and technological resources are used for students to draw personal meaning, solve problems, and make decisions through active involvement with data." Pausing for a moment, she added, "Students will engage with peers, elders, and younger students in analyzing, researching, evaluating, and taking action on community issues."

A comprehensive curriculum restructuring effort at the Philo Elementary School in Winston-Salem, North Carolina, offers another look at the future. With support from the National Education Association as one of its Mastery in Learning sites, the school is focusing its efforts on resource-based learning. Robert McClure, director of the NEA Mastery in Learning Consortium, said, "The consortium's efforts are focused on narrowing the gap between researchers and practitioners, and a resource-based learning approach provides comfortable ground on which the two groups can explain what is happening to students and how the curriculum can be improved."

Therefore, the purpose of this effort is partly to have personnel from the school interact regularly with faculty from nearby colleges of education. The hope is that what the faculty learns as a result of the curriculum reform at Philo will eventually result in curriculum changes at the colleges so that future graduates will be prepared to participate in resource-based learning programs. The results of efforts like those in New Hampshire and North Carolina will, in turn, provide models for other resource-based learning programs.

SCHOOL ASSESSMENTS

As important as test scores and awards are, they can never tell the whole story of a successful program. Principal

Rhodes commented, "I personally do not get all hung up on test scores. If the parents want to know how their students are doing at our school, we do not mind sharing that information. But we also show them what we are doing to make learning better, and we know resource-based learning is the way to go."

Besides test scores, what else should a school that is making a move to resource-based learning look at and evaluate? Following are some suggestions.

Products. Chapter 2 describes some integrated units of study that were undertaken in schools that have embraced resource-based learning. All of those units had an end product. After students had done research and collected data, they published their results in various forms—ranging from videos to books. In the case of a sixth-grade project on the United Nations, Library Media Specialist Geiger reported that the products were "a series of travel posters that had to include basic information about the countries as well as a map and a national flag of each one." These products, which resulted from the efforts of individuals, small groups, or entire classes, were the tangible evidence of what students had mastered both in content and in information literacy.

Discussing the value and limitless possibilities of such products, Principal Harvey said, "I have seen kids take a topic in which one group made a photo essay, and another group made an 8-mm film. Others made slide tapes, to which they added narratives, and still others made murals." She added, "But everybody in the class ended up doing and having some sort of a piece—some sort of a production piece—that they had done in terms of that project."

Often the products involve writing. For example, at Coralville Central Elementary School in Iowa City, children—under the direction of David Quegg, a classroom teacher—publish a school newspaper called the *Central Planet.* Library Media

Coordinator van Deusen also reported that in that same school, every child publishes one "masterpiece" a year. She explained, "It [the masterpiece] is their product that shows how far they have come with their writing." She went on to explain that the children write the books, bind them, and present them to the principal. At the presentation the students get a certificate with a gold seal on it. The book is then cataloged and officially put into the library. She concluded by saying, "It is at this point that the principal, the media center, and the classroom are all part of this publishing activity." Of course, comparing children's masterpieces over a period of years will also provide a concrete means of assessing growth in information literacy, critical thinking, and writing abilities.

Products such as those just mentioned, of course, offer concrete proof—in and of themselves—not only of students' learning but also of their ability to communicate learning to others. Library Media Specialist Geiger thinks these products are such excellent proofs of learning that she keeps albums of photographs showing students working in the library media center as well as their finished products. She said, "I keep the photo albums in the media center so that when people come through—kids and adults—they can look at them."

Student Self-Assessment. While the teacher and/or the library media specialist may evaluate students' products, the critical thinking skills of students can be further enhanced if they also are involved in evaluating their own and other students' efforts. For example, in describing the process of resource-based learning, Principal Dangremond said, "After students understand the skills involved, they choose a topic—something they are interested in. Then they do all the research to support their topics, make some sort of visual aid—like a poster—and then make an oral presentation to their peers. At that point, their classmates evaluate the individual projects, assessing the extent to which each student has become an 'expert' in each particular field." She concluded by saying, "That is just one example of information power at work." *(Figure 7.1 shows a student self-evaluation form that you may want to adapt for your school.)*

An excellent example of students developing critical thinking skills by assessing their own learning came from a fourth-grade unit on pioneers at the R. B. Fernandez Elementary School in San Antonio. Director Dobrot explained that the school library media specialist, Rosemary McCawley, in cooperation with the children's teacher, first had them read some of Laura Ingalls Wilder's books about pioneers. Then, different groups chose a different aspect of pioneer life—such as environment, survival, food, or clothing—to research. When they were finished, they wrote and illustrated reports.

After the children had shared their reports with their classmates, McCawley had them read the unit on pioneers in their textbooks so that they could evaluate how well they had covered it. Dobrot reported, "The children found the textbook was very narrow in its perception of pioneer life." She added that the children also discovered that some of the textbook's generalizations made about pioneers were not true. "The children realized that they knew more about pioneers than the textbook had told them," Dobrot summarized. "The children were learning to be critical thinkers and to analyze and compare the information they had gathered with the information that was given to them in their textbook."

Curiosity and Eagerness. One of the most frequently spoken words in the interviews for this book was *fun*. The fun reportedly starts when teachers, librarians, and other curriculum specialists get together to plan an integrated resource-based study unit. Then it spreads to the students as they begin to research information on topics of real interest to them.

Director Dobrot, for example, told about a group of

FIGURE 7.1

Student Self-Evaluation Form   Name _____

1. Why did you do this project?

2. What did you do for my part in this project?

3. What did you like best about the project you worked on?

4. What would you do differently next time on your project? How would you improve on what you did?

5. What did you like best in all the finished projects you saw?

6. Do you enjoy working in a group or by yourself? Tell why.

7. What did you see other groups do that you would like to try next time?

8. During the oral presentations, what ideas did other classmates use that you liked?

9. Which resources in the Library Media Center did you feel were the most useful?

10. Would you rather learn more about a subject using the Library Media Center and all of its resources OR just reading a textbook on the subject? Tell why.

From David Loertscher's book *Taxonomies of the School Library Media Program.*
Englewood, CO: Libraries Unlimited, 1988.

fourth graders in San Antonio who became involved in a unit on communities. The unit was based on a storyline about two cousins from Buffalo who were visiting their cousins in San Antonio. For this unit, which had been written by their teacher and the school library media specialist, the fourth graders had to give the cousins a tour of the city and tell them the history of San Antonio. As a result, the students had to learn both the history of the city and how to read a road map.

Continuing her story, Dobrot said, "I was over at the school one day when three fourth grade boys asked their teacher if they could skip recess so that they could continue to work on figuring out the mileage around San Antonio. Now, when have you ever seen fourth-grade boys get so excited about learning that they were willing to give up recess?" Teachers and students having fun while teaching and learning certainly is a strong clue that resource-based learning works.

Lack of Discipline Problems. The interviews also revealed that the resource-based approach to learning eliminates most discipline problems. Information Specialist Carter (Sands), for example, said, "There was a noticeable change in behavior problems because students' interest was held; the children simply were not disruptive any more." She went on to say that although she did not have any "hard, fast numbers," she also believed that the students' attendance improved.

Library Media Specialist Geiger echoed Carter (Sands) when she said, "Kids want to come into the library now; they don't avoid it any longer. In fact, they can't wait to get in here." She added, "This new eagerness is something that you can't really document—other than by seeing the enthusiasm on their faces!"

Director Dobrot agreed. She reported that when she visits the libraries in her district that have embraced resource-based learning, she is constantly amazed by what she sees. She explained, "There's no fooling around when children are working on resource-based units—even when they have been in the library for as long as two hours." She believes that there are no longer any discipline problems because "the kids are so excited about what they're learning." Then she added, "They know they can explore beyond their teachers' questions or the prescribed activities. They can keep asking questions and add their own curiosity to their work. It's amazing!"

The connection between eager, interested students and a lack of discipline problems certainly is not mysterious. If students are genuinely involved in what they are doing, they neither have the time nor the inclination to misbehave. Therefore, decreases in disciplinary problems, though difficult to document, are another indication of a successful resource-based learning program.

NEED FOR ADDITIONAL ASSESSMENT

If you are thinking about initiating a move toward resource-based learning, it is essential that from the outset you establish an on-site evaluation program. Documentation of the results of such a program is important for several reasons, but the most important one is that you will need it to help you make future budget decisions. For example, unless the leadership in your school district is sure about the effectiveness of resource-based learning, you may never get the support needed for library media center resources and staffing.

As you are well aware, there is always a strong, emotional pull to sacrifice library media centers and other support services in order to maintain the smallest possible student-to-teacher ratio in the classroom. Only hard data on student performance that can be shared with parents and other concerned individuals can refute such long-held assumptions that class size is THE most important determinant of quality education.

Back in 1976, for example, when the first of many educational budget cuts took place in New York City, only

Community School District #16 in Brooklyn had professional librarians in all of its elementary schools. Those positions, consequently, were in immediate jeopardy. The district is located in a black area where student performance might have been assumed to be poor, and library media programs had so improved students' drop-out rate and grades that school administrators, teachers, and parents rallied to retain the professional librarians in each of the schools. They even held a conference that documented the value of their school library media programs. One of the outcomes of that conference was a publication, which unfortunately is now out-of-print. That booklet, however, was the precursor of this book. Without using the terms *information literacy* and *resource-based learning*, the articles in the booklet documented the benefits of integrating school library programs and resources into classroom learning.

Although emphasis may vary from school to school, the following outline may serve as a basis for an evaluation program. Note that some of the items assume the availability of baseline data from before the move to resource-based learning and/or that cooperative data-sharing with other schools is available.

Academic Performance
1. Changes in overall student performance on standardized tests.
2. Changes in high school graduation rates.
3. Changes in student readiness for and performance in middle and/or high schools.

Individual Student Performance
1. Changes in attendance.
2. Comparison of student papers and projects with those of earlier years or those at "sister" schools that are not involved with resource-based learning.
3. Evidence of students being engaged in critical thinking and self-evaluation.

Those items that will be easiest to assess in terms of the changes caused by resource-based learning are those for which records are already consistently being kept, e.g., standardized tests, graduation rates, and attendance. Next will be those items for which student performance records (e.g., grade point averages) in middle and high schools are available so that they can be compared with the records of students from other elementary schools that do not have resource-based learning.

It is more difficult to compare learning outcomes and higher-order thinking skills because, unfortunately, evaluation in these areas has not been tracked or correlated in most schools, nor is there a tradition of comparative evaluations of students' performances other than on standardized tests. Perhaps the best hope for such comparative evaluations lies within a school or school district where not all classes or schools are involved in resource-based learning. In such cases, comparisons of students' work should be somewhat easier to accomplish.

In addition, portfolio assessment promises to be an effective tool to measure student progress. This technique is presently receiving particular attention as a way to evaluate both students and faculty. Indeed, student portfolios are one of the very best ways to assess students' growth in information literacy, critical thinking, and communication abilities.

In portfolio assessment, samples of students' best work are collected throughout a school year—or throughout all of elementary school—to provide "snapshots" of the students' abilities. By comparing these written, visual, and/or audio products, teachers and principals can track students' performance levels. Although many elementary teachers have been using portfolios in their classrooms for some years now, the research for this book revealed that no schools used portfolio assessment schoolwide. However, pursuing such a method of evaluation is not only possible but also quite desirable.

In many of the interviews for this book, principals and media specialists also shared informal methods of evaluation that revealed the impact of resource-based learning. Library

Media Specialist Coatney, for example, reported that the "kids from our school are better prepared to work with one another at the middle schools, and they also like to read more." Similarly, Principal Thormeyer reported, "Part of the proof that resource-based learning works is that our school had the largest number of children in the summer reading program at the public library last year."

There is one word of caution. Since it takes time to develop in-service training programs, to build collections, and to get the "bugs" worked out of new endeavors, it would be unrealistic to expect overnight improvements in scores on formal tests. For example, when reporting that the fifth-grade writing scores had increased 14 points in her school in San Antonio, Principal Rhodes warned that although she considered this gain to be a dramatic increase, she and her staff were cautious about making overall assessments too early. She pointed out, "The research that we have done indicates that when you move to a resource-based approach, you might actually take an initial drop in scores because your teachers are not drilling on basic skills by drilling for the test." She went on to say, "Over the long term, however, you will see a steady increase in the scores, and you'll also see that the teaching in your school is producing learning instead of just getting students to pass a test. That is what I'm interested in."

However, whether you look at the hard data or the anecdotal reports of school personnel, the results always seem to be the same: Resource-based learning works for students, their parents, their teachers, and—of course—their principals. Perhaps Principal Thormeyer's to-the-point assessment of resource-based learning summed it up best: "Any doubting Thomases should visit a school like ours!"

CHAPTER 8
MOVING FORWARD

> "School leaders must come to understand the changing role of the library and the potential the library media center has for significant improvement of education."
>
> JAMES C. THOMPSON, SUPERINTENDENT OF THE GRAPEVINE-COLLEYVILLE INDEPENDENT SCHOOL DISTRICT, GRAPEVINE, TX

ONE OF THE MOST FRUSTRATING ASPECTS OF ATTENDING a good professional conference is how seldom any concrete results follow. The reason for lack of change, of course, is easy to understand. When you return to your school, the work that has piled up while you were away demands your immediate attention. By the time your workload has reached its normal level, the details of the inspiring session(s) that made the conference exciting to you have dimmed. Moreover, when you finally discuss with your colleagues the ideas that stimulated you a week or two earlier, they appear a bit flat in the translation. Perhaps the greatest deterrent to positive change, however, is the lack of a ready answer to the question: Can what I heard about at the conference really work here in my school?

This chapter is devoted to answering that question about resource-based learning. While every situation is different, the experiences of those interviewed for this book and others have offered some guidelines and even some practical hints that you can use immediately as a starting point for your own efforts.

BEGIN WITH YOURSELF

You need to begin with yourself because, as every library media specialist interviewed for this book testified, an understanding and supportive principal is THE most important factor in establishing a successful resource-based learning program. Therefore, before you do anything else, take time for some honest self-reflection. What images come to your mind when you think about the learning that occurs at your school? Is it active and filled with excitement, or is it mostly passive and filled with boredom and disinterest? Bernice Lamkin, Director of Regional Educational Media Center 7 in Holland, Michigan, urged all educators to consider the process of education that is taking place in their schools when she said, "So many schools aren't dealing with the process in which kids are involved at all today. Schools just sit the kids down and then put a funnel in and pour in all the facts and figures and content. They make sure the kids don't get up and get their hands on anything." Then she added, "But resource-based learning automatically says that the kids have to put their hands on things; they're going to have to go out in all directions and start looking for answers."

Also think long and hard about how well your school's approach to learning is preparing your students for the next century. Director Dobrot pulled no punches when she said,

"One of the most important things that principals have to realize is what today's kids are facing in the 21st century . . . . If kids don't know they need information and if they don't know how to find information, they're not going to be successful." Then Dobrot paused and asked, "What is our society then going to do to take care of these people who don't know how to take care of themselves educationally?"

Realizing that the stakes are so high, James C. Thompson, while superintendent of the Blue Valley School District in Overland Park, Kansas, also warned in an article in the May 1991 *NASSP Bulletin* that educators need to reexamine their concepts of what school library media centers are and what they are capable of accomplishing.

> Many school leaders have difficulty in recognizing the potential benefits of resource-based learning because their school library paradigm is one based upon the traditional view of the school library. These leaders remember the school library as a repository of books and materials that was closely guarded and monitored by non-smiling book shelvers whose job seemed to be to keep the place quiet and unused. A visit to the library meant a scheduled 20-minute search for a novel, or quiet reading time, and many schools used the space for study hall. . . . [p. 25]

In the statement that begins this chapter, Superintendent Thompson issues an appeal to his readers: "School leaders must come to understand the changing role of the library and the potential the library media center has for significant improvement of education." [p. 25]

Obviously, your own paradigm must shift before you can begin to sway others' traditional view of the school library and of learning in general. Principal Rhodes summed up the importance of a principal's attitude when she emphasized that "the principal must believe that there is a better way for children to learn."

One of the best ways to speed up your paradigm shift is to find out more about resource-based learning. Read some of the sources mentioned in the Selected Reading List on pages 150–152 and attend as many workshops and conferences on this subject that you can. Most of all, however, you need to get first-hand experiences with resource-based learning by spending a morning or an afternoon at a school that is using this approach. Observe the interactive activities of the children, take note of their involved expressions, and listen to the enthusiasm in their voices. If you do not know how to locate a resource-based library media program in your area, write a note of inquiry to the Executive Director of the American Association of School Librarians, 50 E. Huron St., Chicago, IL 60611. You also may want to contact some of the principals quoted in this book and arrange to meet them at the next conference of the National Association of Elementary School Principals.

DEVELOP A VISION

According to Superintendent Thompson, the next step in moving toward resource-based learning at your school is to consider where the process will lead you.

> What is the end result that is desired? This desired end should be seen in terms of learning benefits. Once the vision has been developed, it should be shared by the leader and infused into the basic framework of the school. The leader should promote the concept of resource-based learning in all possible settings. As the organization comes to recognize the importance of the approach, the basic vision can be espoused in a policy statement and in the school's long- and short-term goals. [pp. 26–27]

For Thompson, the learning benefits that were ultimately desired for students boiled down to three overriding priorities: to find and analyze information, to work cooperatively, and to communicate well.

Setting such priorities is the purpose of mission statements. In the collection of materials received from various schools involved in resource-based learning, the following philosophy and mission statement from the Richmond School in Sussex, Wisconsin, stands out as a model well worth imitating.

> We believe in the inherent worth of each individual, and in his/her capacity for intellectual, social, cultural, and physical growth. However, because variations exist in individual needs and potentials, we deem it vital that a continuing effort be made to provide for these differences in our total school program.
>
> We believe that the development of personality, emotional maturity, physical and mental health, and civic, social, and economic living should be interwoven into the fabric of each individual's total education.
>
> We believe that the basic skills of reading, writing, speaking, listening, thinking, computing, and evaluating are fundamental to learning in all educational areas.
>
> We believe in the development of a student who will be an independent, self-reliant seeker of knowledge, one who can ask increasingly original and relevant questions about himself/herself and about the society in which he/she lives.
>
> We believe another important aim of our school is to develop each individual's capacity to assume more and more responsibility for his/her own education since his/her development must not cease when the student's formal education has ended.
>
> We believe, in the final analysis, that a sense of relevance and flexibility must pervade our school's educational philosophy and objectives if we are to implement the new ideas of the future as well as the wisdom of the past.

The very process of developing such a mission statement with the involvement of school personnel, parents, and community leaders can go a long way toward building awareness of the value of resource-based learning. Any thoughtful consideration of how to achieve goals such as "[to develop] a student who will be an independent, self-reliant seeker of knowledge" and "to develop each individual's capacity to assume more and more responsibility for his/her own education" must eventually lead to an integration of learning resources into the curriculum. Therefore, the process of developing the mission statement itself can become a significant energizing factor in moving toward resource-based learning.

Information Power, a pilot project in Michigan, provides a model mission statement for library media programs and highlights the importance of such a statement. Ideally, however, the philosophy of resource-based learning should permeate the mission statement of a school rather than being part of a separate mission statement for the library media center. Such an approach makes absolutely clear that the library media program is integral to the mission of the entire school.

INTRODUCE THE VISION

While you are developing a mission statement, or even earlier, you can undertake other practical initiatives to engage your teachers' interest in resource-based learning. For example, the following four steps can improve teachers' understanding of resource-based learning and information literacy and encourage their adoption into the curriculum.

Inform and Explore. Share with your teachers a few carefully selected professional articles on resource-based learning and provide an opportunity for teachers to discuss them. Explore what teachers liked about the concepts and practices showcased in the articles. Find out what they feel might be barriers to implementation. Principal Dangremond described this process at her school when she said, "I listened, listened, listened. I constantly communicated, constantly reassured the teachers that it was all right that we were going through this chaos—this feeling of confusion." Then she added. "As much as possible, I also provided research articles so that they [the teachers] would have the background. We talked in small groups because there's some comfort knowing that other people are going through the same thing you are going through."

Model Resource-Based Learning. In-service programs that highlight examples of resource-based learning already in place within your school—or if need be, at a nearby school—are extremely beneficial. Let teachers "sell" the concept to other teachers, based on their own experiences and enthusiasm. Principal Harvey, for example, emphasized the need for working models by saying, "One problem I see is that we often have very little modeling of resource-based learning for teachers to actually see what is involved in the process. They need to see for themselves, for example, what is going to happen and how kids will really begin to take ownership of their learning. They also need to see how much more in-depth kids will go in terms of learning when they are given the opportunity." She concluded by stressing, "Unless teachers are able to see a model, it will be very difficult for them to walk into their classrooms and take risks."

Provide a Vocabulary. Providing a working vocabulary for resource-based learning should prove to be very helpful as you talk to and educate not only your teachers but also other administrative personnel. You, of course, will show the importance you place on resource-based learning by always discussing it and highlighting its goals and outcomes. Director

Lamkin reported that in her district in Michigan, "We ask the principals to bring resource-based learning up at every teachers' meeting. It needs to become the vocabulary of the building." She added, "For example, both of our resource-based pilot projects have names. One is *Information Power* and the other is *Information Is Power.* Each school chose its own name because a name is helpful; it gives substance."

Explain Empowerment. Finally, help your teachers understand how resource-based learning, rather than being just another fad, can empower them to improve the quality of learning. Principal Dangremond, in particular, emphasized the importance of this step. She advised that one of the tactics that worked best for her was emphasizing how the changes pay off for the students. As a result, she kept telling her teachers to ask, "What is best for the children?"

BUILD SUPPORT FOR THE VISION

Once you have a good sense of how your teachers are going to react to curriculum revisions based on resource-based learning, you can determine to a large degree how much time and effort it will take to create a climate conducive to curriculum reform. Following, therefore, are six suggestions for encouraging a climate for change in your school.

Be Patient. Do not rush acceptance, but be firm in your commitment. Principal Dangremond confirmed this need for patience when she stated the following in her interview.

> You have to be patient and understanding. You also have to be committed to the project, willing, for example, to provide some financial support. More than anything else, though, you have to be willing to give of your time, and it takes a tremendous amount of principal time!

You also have to accept the fact that teachers will work through the process at different rates and in different ways. You also have to expect some crisis points along the way, but you have to have some confidence that your staff will be able to work through them. In addition, you must allow for some trial and error because you can't just hand your teachers the package and insist they use it. If you do that, they're never going to have ownership of the project. It'll just become an add-on.

On the other hand, as the principal, you have to appear confident and self-assured, but you also have to make it perfectly clear that it's not going to go away—that you are not going to go back to the old way.

Provide Planning Time. Ensure that the library media specialist and teachers have opportunities to meet to develop curriculum units. Principal Rhodes explained that team planning took on new meaning when resource-based learning was at its core. She explained, "Before, team planning meant that we met to iron out logistics. Now it means brainstorming, identifying resources, and allocating time." With great enthusiasm she continued, "It means who is going to do what; how is this unit going to fit into our overall objective; how do math, reading, social studies, and science fit into this unit; and how can we work in parental involvement. We are truly developing a whole program!"

Offer Plenty of Staff Development. From the beginning, offer ample opportunities for staff development so that teachers—and the library media specialist, if necessary—can gain the self-confidence they need to work collaboratively with others and to incorporate more learning resources into their classes. *(For more information about staff development, see Chapter 4.)*

Provide Incentives. Provide incentives for resource-based learning projects—such as cash, equipment, or materials. As mentioned in Chapter 4, several principals stated up front that if their teachers were doing a project or unit with the library media specialist, they would provide additional monies for supplies or materials. Principal Dangremond commented that under such circumstances, even some non-risk-taking teachers were willing to try a pilot project.

Begin Pilot Programs. Start small with only one integrated resource-based project per grade level, or start big with a whole grade level. Just start somewhere. One of the major advantages of pilot projects is that they allow change to occur gradually with only one or a few of the more enterprising teachers. Pilots also allow less adventuresome teachers to see the benefits of this approach at close range before they are asked to modify their own teaching practices. Pilots also allow time for support to build within the school and among parents. Retired Library Media Specialist Pacholl urged even nonbelievers to give resource-based learning a fair trial when he said, "If you give resource-based learning/integrated instruction a fair and honest trial, you'll have to agree that it is far superior to the traditional textbook approach and the traditional library media approach."

Use Evaluation As an Instrument for Change. Consider making the integration of information resources into the curriculum part of your teacher evaluation criteria. Principal Dangremond underscored the need to use yearly evaluations in this manner to provide an important "incentive" for teachers to get involved with resource-based learning. Principal Rhodes also emphasized the importance of striving for teacher ownership and leadership. She explained as follows.

> It used to be that instead of taking responsibility as the coordinator of learning, teachers would rely on the librarian to set a time and a course of action for what students would be doing in the library.

Resource-based learning puts teachers back into a decision-making mode of planning ahead, coordinating, and thinking about their students' needs and how the library can fit in. The library must become a place where teachers all go and interact with the media specialist for a particular purpose. This is a shift that has to be made.

However, it is unlikely that such a shift will take place unless teachers know that they will be held accountable for effectively incorporating information resources into their curriculum. Specifically stated, expectations are clearly an effective way of getting teachers' attention. Positive experiences—even with initially "coerced" efforts—should quickly lead to more positive motivations for pursuing resource-based learning.

OBTAIN THE VISION

Much has already been said in this book about collaborative planning and collaborative learning. Resource-based learning requires partnering between teachers and library media specialists, between them and students, and among the learners themselves. The single most effective thing you can do to create a climate for such activities is to model such partnering. As the principal, you can demonstrate the benefits and overall value of collaborative efforts by partnering with the library media specialist. Together you can become the dynamic duo that provides the vision, the drive, and the support that makes recourse-based learning an exciting alternative to "business as usual."

Such a partnership makes good sense from several perspectives. First of all, only you and the library media specialist are responsible for all the children across the entire curriculum and throughout the entire time they are at your school. Second, only you and the library media specialist are concerned about balancing limited resources across all subject areas. Third, such a partnership forms a solid basis for mutual support, planning, and evaluation.

Finally and most importantly, the on-going, mutually supportive relationship between you and your library media specialist, which will be discussed more fully later in this chapter, will become a model for the kind of partnerships that need to be developed at the teacher/specialist level *(see Figure 8.1)*. Moreover, while resource-based learning programs are being established, collaborative meetings can be both an effective means of timely trouble-shooting and tangible proof that the new endeavor has all of your support.

Indeed, the most successful resource-based programs testify to the importance and effectiveness of the principal/library media specialist partnership, for each considers the other to be the key to success. Principal Dangremond, for example, said without hesitation, "I happen to have a library media specialist who is wonderful at creating the vision. She is very creative, a dreamer; and we work together beautifully as a team, because I can add that touch of reality that is needed to complete a project."

Therefore, after you model a partnering relationship, the next most important thing is to create partnerships between the teachers and the library media specialist. Library Media Specialist Ellen Tirone explained how this partnership developed at her school in New Hampshire.

> With some reluctance, skepticism, and "unwarranted optimism," a handful of Harold Martin School teachers piloted a new approach to developing a unit of study with the library media professional in the winter of 1990. Support by the principal in providing the gift of time and the risk of failure enabled these educators to forge into new territory. Armed with diverse personalities and teaching styles, the newly formed partnership experienced laughing, worrying, and sharing stress together. They fostered a mutual

FIGURE 8.1

PARTNERSHIP NEEDED FOR A SUCCESSFUL LIBRARY MEDIA PROGRAM

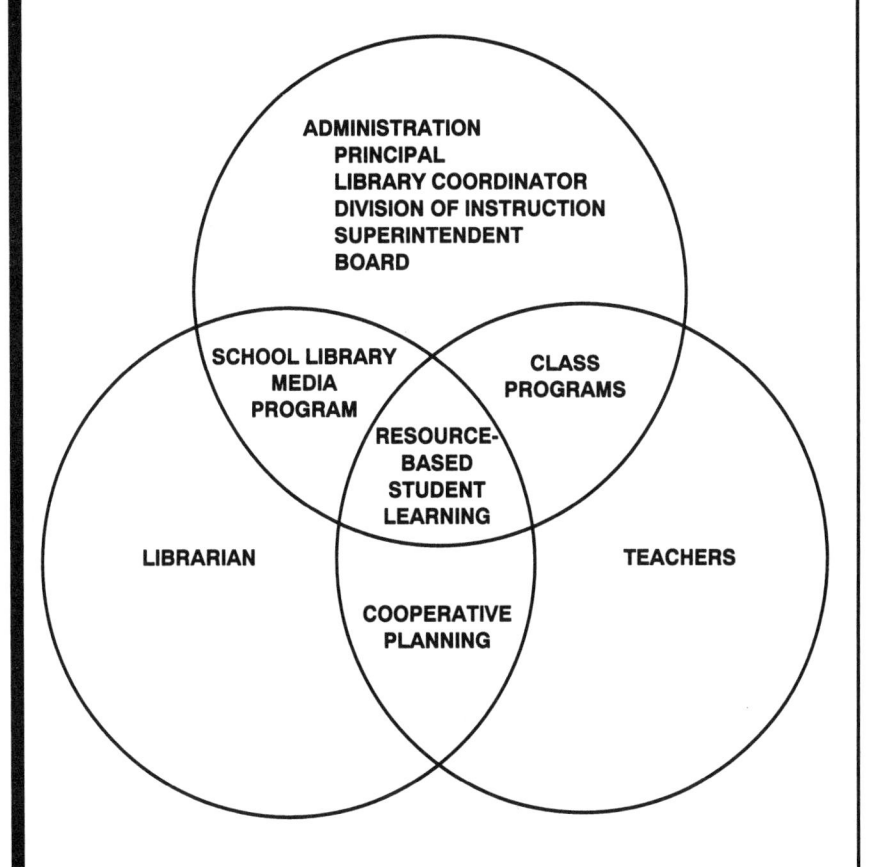

ADMINISTRATION
PRINCIPAL
LIBRARY COORDINATOR
DIVISION OF INSTRUCTION
SUPERINTENDENT
BOARD

SCHOOL LIBRARY MEDIA PROGRAM

CLASS PROGRAMS

RESOURCE-BASED STUDENT LEARNING

LIBRARIAN

TEACHERS

COOPERATIVE PLANNING

Nancy L. Dobrot and Rosemary McCawley. *Beyond Flexible Scheduling,* ©1992, Hi Willow Research and Publishing/67 respect of ideas and relied on individual strengths to develop and coordinate a unit. This first taste of grade level cooperative planning helped moved individuals beyond uncertainties and trepidations to a mutual sense of excitement and collegiality!...An important by-product of this process is a cohesive group of educators impacting the school with increased sensitivity, cooperation, and communication.

Principals and supervisors also spoke about the importance of the teacher/media specialist team. Principal Dangremond, for example, referred to the teachers and media specialist as "the co-designers of the curriculum, with the media specialist as the resource specialist and the teacher as the contents specialist—both working together." Library Media Coordinator van Deusen echoed this sentiment by saying, "In our schools we encourage the teachers and media specialists to plan together because we believe the notion that two heads are better than one."

Also important in fostering team relationships is the ability of your media specialist to schedule flexible library schedules, which was discussed in Chapter 4. Such schedules are important because they provide the time for teachers and media specialists to work and plan together. Another benefit of flexible schedules occurs after teachers start to come into the library with their students—willingly or unwillingly. They begin to get a sense of shared ownership.

Van Deusen summed it up when she said, "The notion of sending kids off to the media center from the classroom and the teacher never seeing what happens there is a real problem because classroom teachers can't develop a view of what a media specialist can do unless they see it and become a part of it themselves. That shared ownership, I think, is a necessary ingredient in making resource-based learning work."

The importance of making time for such collaborations is also documented in a report by the Colorado Department of Education. *(For other details of this report, see Chapter 5.)*

> The degree of collaboration between library media specialist and teachers is affected by the ratio of teachers to pupils. Collaboration of this type depends on the availability of both media specialist and teacher to engage in this important work. Specialists who play an instructional role tend to have teacher-colleagues whose workloads also permit such collaboration. [p. 96]

The partnering needed for successful resource-based learning programs, in fact, includes even students. *Information Power* devotes several pages to each partner's role in building successful school library media programs. Following is the beginning of that discussion.

> An effective school library media program depends on the collaborative efforts of all those who are responsible for student learning. The coordination of curriculum development and implementation with the resources of the school library media center, and the application of principles of information access to the content of the curriculum, provide the basis for an effective program. In effect, all members of the educational community, including teachers, principals, students, and library media specialists, become partners in a shared goal—providing successful learning experiences for all students. [pp. 21–22]

Once these important relationships of resource-based learning are in place, you are sure to make progress and the evidence of this progress will be the growth and excitement that will occur for everyone involved. Expressing this excitement, Principal Rhodes said, "Resource-based learning is helping educators move back to teaching the whole child." She paused and then continued, "But it's more than that. It is challenging children, challenging teachers, and challenging all of us as learners to extend beyond the basics into critical thinking skills, because an integrated curriculum means that children learn the basics and then do something about them!"

Ultimately, therefore, one of the best outcomes of a resource-based learning program is the empowerment of students to step into the partnership of learners. As Rhodes said, "A program is successful when students start taking more responsibility for their own learning."

Possess the Rewards of the Vision

Throughout this book you have been continually reminded of the present and lifelong benefits resource-based learning offers to children, but until now the issue of "what's in it for you?" has not been directly addressed. As the key player in making resource-based learning take hold in your school, you will become an instructional leader par excellence! Looking back and reflecting on her own experience, Principal Rhodes shared the changes that have occurred in her life since the teachers in her school embraced resource-based learning.

> I truly feel that I am able to be the kind of principal that we all dream about—not that I have achieved that entirely, but my teachers accept responsibility for their work; they plan well together and they work well together. I have become an instructional leader, and in that capacity I am sort of a cheerleader for all of them. I try to sit back and listen, and when we set goals, I try to help to see if we can realistically achieve them.
>
> I think that is the role of the principal, as the instructional leader: to be a visionary, to always have that vision clear, and to help move toward that vision. The teachers are doing it, but I am there to help them overcome the obstacles, which may be finances, schedules, communication with parents, or communication with each other. That is what I came into administration to do—not to manage a building and not to sit in my office and make wonderful schedules that make everything look smooth and wonderful—but to help teachers help children to learn. It is very exciting for me.

Do you feel that same excitement? Are you confident that in your role as instructional leader you really are helping your teachers help their students learn? Can you—like Principal Dangremond—be sure that your school is "producing people who will be lifelong learners, good problem solvers, self-directed individuals, effective communicators, technologically literate adults, and collaborative contributors"? She warned, however, that "this isn't just going to happen. It will require leadership." Are you ready to provide that leadership at your school so that all of your Calvins do not have to go through too many more "typical" days at school?

CALVIN AND HOBBES copyright 1993 Watterson.
Dist. by UNIVERSAL PRESS SYNDICATE. Reprinted with permission. All rights reserved.

You have already taken a major step toward resource-based learning by reading this book. Now there is one question left for you to answer: *Where will your next step take you—and all of the children in your school?*

CLOSING THOUGHTS

AS THE FINISHING TOUCHES WERE BEING ADDED TO THE manuscript for this book, we were already sensing a great frustration at not being able to include as many stories and issues as we had wanted. Left out, for example, was the discussion of the importance of attractive, well thought out facilities, including Library Media Specialist Coatney's description of her library as "extremely beautiful with toys and huge stuffed animals everywhere . . . a real children's kind of place."

The omission of bigger issues, of course, caused even greater frustration. For example, we had wanted very much to be able to share with you the 1992 publication of the State University of New York entitled *SUNY 2000: College Expectations: The Report of the SUNY Task Force on College Entry-Level Knowledge and Skills* because it recommends that teacher education and library school curricula incorporate strong information literacy components so that all school teachers and librarians will be able to integrate information skills into their work with students. The task force stated its rationale for the latter by saying, "In the belief that any form of 'two-tiered society' must be avoided, we advocate the goal of information literacy for all high school graduates, not merely those with imminent plans to attend college."

Most of all, however, we regretted not being able to share the wealth and maturity of resource-based learning programs in other countries such as Australia, Canada, and Great Britain. In Australia, for instance, a wide range of national documents underscore the need for an information-literate citizenry and for schools to provide appropriate curriculums to that end. As a result, almost every state in Australia has an information literacy curriculum guide, supplemented by other helpful materials. Similarly, in the Netherlands there is a national curriculum requirement that will enable all students to acquire information literacy by their early teens. Based upon information like this, it would seem that although the United States may still be the leader among the Western information societies, it is behind a number of other countries in assuring that its future citizens will be well prepared to help their country maintain its position of world leadership.

In spite of our frustrations, we finished this book with an optimistic feeling about the future of the United States. Because of the creativity, determination, and talents demonstrated by the educational leaders quoted in this book, we feel sure that future generations of information-literate school graduates will be well equipped for lifelong learning and productivity in the workplace. We also hope that soon it can be said that all school graduates are well prepared to seek and find the truth—for it is only the truth that shall make them free and keep them free.

The Authors

SELECTED READING LIST

- American Association of School Librarians. *Information Literacy: Learning How to Learn.* Chicago, IL: American Library Association, 1991.

    (This publication is made up of a collection of articles from *School Library Media Quarterly*, the official journal of this organization. The overall emphasis of the 17 articles is on the role of resource-based learning in developing higher-order thinking skills. All of the articles may be photocopied for the noncommercial purpose of scientific or educational advancement; they also can serve as good discussion pieces for staff development activities.)

- American Association of School Librarians and Association for Educational Communicators and Technology. *Information Power: Guidelines for School Library Media Programs.* Chicago, IL: American Library Association, 1988.

    (All aspects of a building-level library media program are covered in these guidelines.)

- *American Library Association Presidential Committee on Information Literacy: Final Report.* Chicago, IL: American Library Association, January 1989.

    (This publication, which was written by national leaders in education and librarianship, is the foundation document on information literacy. A definition of an information literate person is included, and the ramifications of information literacy on individual lives, businesses, and citizenship are outlined. See Appendix A for the entire text. Duplication is permitted, or single free copies of the printed version may be obtained by writing to the American Library Association, 50 East Huron St., Chicago, IL 60611.)

- Carletti, Silvana, Suzanne Girad, and Katheleen Willing. *The Library/Classroom Connection.* Portsmouth, NH: Heinemann Educational Books, Inc., 1991.

    (This book gives practical advice for getting teachers and library media specialists to work together to develop resource-based learning programs.)

- Dobrot, Nancy L., and Rosemary McCawley. *Beyond Flexible Scheduling: A Workshop Guide.* Castle Rock, CO: Hi Willow Research and Publishing, 1992.

    (This practical guide provides hands-on help in integrating a library media program into the curriculum and in facilitating staff development so that the integration will be successful. Materials may be reproduced for workshop presentations.)

- Eisenberg, Michael B., and Robert E. Berkowitz. *Information Problem-Solving: The Big Six Skills Approach to Library and Information Skills Instruction.* Norwood, NJ: Ablex Publishing Corp., 1990.

    (Written by a college professor and a library media specialist, this book, which builds on their 1988 book, presents the concept of a general problem-solving approach to library and information skills instruction and explains the information skills that accompany it. Their 1988 book, *Curriculum Initiative: An Agenda for Library Media Programs,* provides a framework and practical approach to curriculum-related responsibilities of library media programs.)

- ERIC Clearinghouse on Information Resources is the publishing partner of the National Forum on Information Literacy.

    (For information on how to obtain other ERIC materials on information literacy, call ACCESSERIC, 1-800-LET-ERIC, or contact a public or academic library.)

- Fredericks, Anthony D. *The Integrated Curriculum: Books for Reluctant Readers, Grades 2-5*. Englewood, CO: Teacher Ideas Press, 1992.

    (This book grows out of a teacher's 20 years of experience and reflects projects and activities that "were generated, proposed, and used by students." The opening section provides a rich compilation of ideas on how to motivate students to read and how to increase their comprehension. The bulk of the publication, however, provides detailed suggestions on how to integrate 39 different books into the curriculum.)

- Haycock, Ken, ed. *Program Advocacy: Power, Publicity, and the Teacher-Librarian*. Englewood, CO: Libraries Unlimited, 1990.

    (These publications consist of compilations of selected articles from *Emergency Librarian* that relate to the changing role of what the Canadians call the teacher-librarian.)

- Jay, M. Ellen and Hilda L. Jay. *Designing Instruction for Diverse Abilities and the Library Media Teacher's Role*. Hamden, CT: Library Professional Publication, 1991.

    (This publication provides materials designed for individuals or small groups for differentiated instruction and individualized access to information.)

- Krashen, Stephen. *The Power of Reading: Insights from the Research*. Englewood, Co: Libraries Unlimited, 1993.

    (This publication summarizes research studies of the nineteenth and twentieth centuries that have explored (1) the power of voluntary reading to increase literacy, (2) the elements necessary to promote voluntary reading, and (3) other factors involved in voluntary reading and literacy, such as television viewing.)

- Lance, Keith Curry, Lynda Welborn, and Christine Hamilton-Pennell. *The Impact of School Library Media Centers on Academic Achievement*. Englewood, CO: Libraries Unlimited, 1993.

    (This book reports on over 40 research studies in the past 30 years that have focused on the impact of school libraries on academic achievement. Some of the findings in this book are reprinted in Appendix G of this book.)

- Loertscher, David. *Taxonomies of the School Library Media Program*. Englewood, CO: Libraries Unlimited, 1988.

    (This book spells out the different levels of library media services and the effects those levels have on learning. Taxonomies are also provided for principals, teachers, and library media specialists. Worksheets are included for planning, materials needed, lesson evaluation, student questionnaires, and other areas.)

- McElmeel, Sharron L. *Bookpeople: A Multicultural Album*. Englewood, CO: Teacher Ideas Press, 1992.

    (This publication is designed to offer practical suggestions for integrating literature and multicultural activities. The introduction states the purpose of the author/illustrator: "Where the bookperson represents a culture or heritage unfamiliar to the reader...[it] helps develop an understanding and appreciation of that heritage or culture"; for the other students it can serve as a validation of their cultural background.)

- Mohr, Carolyn, Dorothy Nixon, and Shirley Vickers. *Books that Heal: A Whole Language Approach*. Englewood, CO: Teacher Ideas Press, 1991.
  (The authors provide structured guides to 24 fiction books that can be used to help children identify with others who have coped with situations similar to ones they are confronting. Topics include death, differences, divorce, poverty, relationships, and self-concept.)

- *NASSP Bulletin* "Restructuring and School Libraries," 75:535. May 1991.
  (This issue contains nine articles on resource-based learning. Although they are targeted at the middle school and secondary levels, most of the concepts can easily be adapted to the elementary school setting. Authors include James C. Thompson, superintendent of the Blue Valley School District in Overland Park, KS; Tim Westerberg, principal of Littleton High School in Littleton, CO; Carol-Ann Haycock, trainer and staff development consultant at the Human Resources Development Group in Vancouver, B.C., and others.)

- Nimon, Maureen and Ann Hazell, eds. *Promoting Learning: Challenges in Teacher Librarianship*. Adelaide, Australia: Auslib Press, 1990.
  (This book contains 16 articles by Australian writers on library media programs in that country including Gloria Rolton's article "Literature and Learning," which is highlighted in Chapter 3 of this book.)

- Pacholl, Dean F. *Integrated Instruction in Elementary School*. Austin, MN: DFP Press (604 5th Ave., SW), 1992.
  (This book for classroom teachers and library media specialists provides ideas and models for integrated units for K-5. It also comes with an Appleworks data disk.)

- *Phi Delta Kappan,* 73:7, March 1992.
  (This issue contains six articles related to the role of library media programs in restructuring schools toward resource-based learning, promoting reading and whole language programs, and promoting school readiness. It also contains the Jack W. Humphrey article that was highlighted in Chapter 3 of this book.)

- Snibbe, Jane. *SCI-TIES: Literature-based Thematic Science Units*. The School Librarian's Workshop 10, (October 1989): 6-10.
  (This sample lesson makes the whole language, literature-based, resource-based education connection. Following the *California Literature Project model,* two sample units are outlined: whales at the primary level and machines at the intermediate level.)

- Stripling, Barbara K. *Libraries for the National Education Goals*. Syracuse, NY: ERIC Clearinghouse on Information Resources, April 1992.
  (This summation of information about the role of public and school libraries in a vast number of educational efforts provides evidence of how library programs support the National Education Goals.)

- Stripling, Barbara K. and Judy M. Pitts. *Brainstorms and Blueprints: Teaching Library Research as a Thinking Process*. Englewood, CO: Libraries Unlimited, 1988.
  (The book provides a six-step taxonomy of thoughtful research: fact-finding, asking/searching, examining/ organizing, evaluating/deliberating, integrating/concluding, and conceptualizing. Activities are suggested that correspond to the taxonomies, and each of the taxonomies is connected to specific student behaviors.)

APPENDIX A

AMERICAN LIBRARY ASSOCIATION PRESIDENTIAL COMMITTEE ON INFORMATION LITERACY: FINAL REPORT

No other change in American society has offered greater challenges than the emergence of the Information Age. Information is expanding at an unprecedented rate, and enormously rapid strides are being made in the technology for storing, organizing, and accessing the ever growing tidal wave of information. The combined effect of these factors is an increasingly fragmented information base—large components of which are only available to people with money and/or acceptable institutional affiliations.

Yet in an information society all people should have the right to information which can enhance their lives. Out of the superabundance of available information, people need to be able to obtain specific information to meet a wide range of personal and business needs. These needs are largely driven either by the desire for personal growth and advancement or by the rapidly changing social, political, and economic environments of American society. What is true today is often outdated tomorrow. A good job today may be obsolete next year. To promote economic independence and quality of existence, there is a lifelong need for being informed and up-to-date.

How our country deals with the realities of the Information Age will have enormous impact on our democratic way of life and on our nation's ability to compete internationally. Within America's information society, there also exists the potential of addressing many long-standing social and economic inequities. To reap such benefits, people—as individuals and as a nation—must be information literate. To be information literate, a person must be able to recognize when information is needed and have the ability to locate, evaluate, and use effectively the needed information. Producing such a citizenry will require that schools and colleges appreciate and integrate the concept of information literacy into their learning programs and that they play a leadership role in equipping individuals and institutions to take advantage of the opportunities inherent within the information society.

Ultimately, information literate people are those who have learned how to learn. They know how to learn because they know how knowledge is organized, how to find information, and how to use information in such a way that others can learn from them. They are people prepared for lifelong learning, because they can always find the information needed for any task or decision at hand.

THE IMPORTANCE OF INFORMATION LITERACY TO INDIVIDUALS, BUSINESS, AND CITIZENSHIP
In Individuals' Lives

Americans have traditionally valued quality of life and the pursuit of happiness; however, these goals are increasingly difficult to achieve because of the complexities of life in today's information and technology dependent society. The cultural and educational opportunities available in an average community, for example, are often missed by people who lack the ability to keep informed of such activities, and lives of information-illiterates are more likely than others to be narrowly focused on second-hand experiences of life through television. On the other hand, life is more interesting when one knows what is going on, what opportunities exist, and where alternatives to current practices can be discovered.

On a daily basis, problems are more difficult to solve when people lack access to meaningful information vital to good decision making. Many people are vulnerable to poorly informed people or opportunists when selecting nursing care for a parent or facing a major expense such as purchasing, financing, or insuring a new home or car. Other information-dependent decisions can affect one's entire lifetime. For example, what information do young people have available to them when they consider which college to attend or whether to become sexually active? Even in areas where one can achieve an expertise, constantly changing and expanding information bases necessitate an ongoing struggle for individuals to keep up-to-date and in control of their daily information environment as well as with information from other fields which can affect the outcomes of their decisions.

In an attempt to reduce information to easily manageable segments, most people have become dependent on others for their information. Information prepackaging in schools and through broadcast and print news media, in fact, encourages people to accept the opinions of others without much thought. When opinions are biased, negative, or inadequate for the needs at hand, many people are left helpless to improve the situation confronting them. Imagine, for example, a family which is being evicted by a landlord who claims he is within his legal rights. Usually they will have to accept the landlord's "expert" opinion, because they do not know how to seek information to confirm or disprove his claim.

Information literacy, therefore, is a means of personal empowerment. It allows people to verify or refute expert opinion and to become independent seekers of truth. It provides them with the ability to build their own arguments and to experience the excitement of the search for knowledge.

It not only prepares them for lifelong learning; but, by experiencing the excitement of their own successful quests for knowledge, it also creates in young people the motivation for pursuing learning throughout their lives.

Moreover, the process of searching and interacting with the ideas and values of their own and others' cultures deepens people's capacities to understand and position themselves within larger communities of time and place. By drawing on the arts, history, and literature of previous generations, individuals and communities can affirm the best in their cultures and determine future goals.

It is unfortunate that the very people who most need the empowerment inherent in being information literate are the least likely to have learning experiences which will promote these abilities. Minority and at-risk students, illiterate adults, people with English as a second language, and economically disadvantaged people are among those most likely to lack access to the information that can improve their situations. Most are not even aware of the potential help that is available to them. Libraries, which provide the best access point to information for most U.S. citizens, are left untapped by those who most need help to improve their quality of life. As former U.S. Secretary of Education Terrell Bell once wrote, "There is a danger of a new elite developing in our country: the information elite."

In Business

Herbert E. Meyer, who has served as an editor for *Fortune* magazine and as vice-chairman of the National Intelligence Council, underscores the importance of access to and use of good information for business in an age characterized by rapid change, a global environment, and unprecedented access to information. In his 1988 book, *Real World Intelligence,* he describes the astonishment and growing distress of executives who "are discovering that the only thing as difficult and dangerous as managing a large enterprise with too little information is managing one with too much" (p. 29).

While Meyer emphasizes that companies should rely on public sources that are available to anyone for much of their information (p. 36), it is clear that many companies do not know how to find and use such information effectively. Every day lack of timely and accurate information is costly to American businesses. The following examples document cases of such losses or near losses.

> A manufacturing company had a research team of three scientists and four technicians working on a project, and at the end of a year the team felt it had a patentable invention in addition to a new product. Prior to filing the patent application, the company's patent attorney requested a literature search. While doing the search, the librarian found that the proposed application duplicated some of the work claimed in a patent that had been issued about a year before the team had begun its work. During the

course of the project, the company had spent almost $500,000 on the project, an outlay that could have been avoided if it had spent the approximately $300 required to have a review of the literature completed before beginning the project.

A manufacturing company was sued by an individual who claimed that the company had stolen his "secret formula" for a product that the company had just marketed. An information scientist on the staff of the company's technical library found a reference in the technical literature that this formula was generally known to the trade long before the litigant developed his "secret formula." When he was presented with this information, the litigant dropped his $7 million claim.

When the technical librarian for an electronics firm was asked to do a literature search for one of its engineers, four people had already been working to resolve a problem for more than a year. The literature search found an article that contained the answer the engineer needed to solve his problem. The article had been published several years before the project team had begun its work. Had the literature search been conducted when the problem was first identified, the company could have saved four man-years of labor and its resulting direct monetary costs.

The need for people in business who are competent managers of information is important at all levels, and the realities of the Information Age require serious rethinking of how businesses should be conducted. Harlan Cleveland explores this theme in his book, *The Knowledge Executive*.

> Information (organized data, the raw material for specialized knowledge, and generalist wisdom) is now our most important and pervasive resource. Information workers now compose more than half the U.S. labor force. But this newly dominant resource is quite unlike the tangible resources we have heretofore thought of as valuable. The differences help explain why we get into so much trouble trying to use for the management of information concepts that worked all right in understanding the management of things—concepts such as control, secrecy, ownership, privilege and geopolitics.

> Because the old pyramids of influence and control were based on just these ideas, they are now crumbling. Their weakening is not always obvious, just as a wooden structure may look solid when you can't see what termites have done to its insides. Whether this "crumble effect" will result in a fairer shake for the world's disadvantaged majority is not yet clear. But there is ample evidence that those who learn now to achieve access to the bath of knowledge that already envelops the world will be the future's aristocrats of achievement, and that they will be far more numerous than any aristocracy in history.

In Citizenship

American democracy has led to the evolution of many thousands of organized citizen groups that seek to influence public policy, issues, and community problems. Following are just a few examples.

> A local League of Women Voters has been chosen to study housing patterns for low-income individuals in its community. It must inform its members of the options for low-income housing and, in the process, comment publicly on the city's long-range, low-income housing plans.

> In an upper midwestern city, one with the highest unemployment rate in 50 years, a major automobile company offers to build a new assembly plant in the central city. The only stipulation is that the city condemn property in a poor ethnic neighborhood of 3,500 residents for use as the site of its plant. In addition, the company seeks a twelve-year tax abatement. Residents of the neighborhood frantically seek to find out how they might save their community from the wrecker's ball but still improve their tax base.

> A group of upper-middle-class women in the Junior League has read about increased incidences of child abuse. They want to become better informed about the elements of child abuse: What brings it on? What incidents have occurred in their own community? What services are available in their community? What actions might they take?

To address these problems successfully, each of these groups will have to secure access to a wide range of information, much of which—if they know how to find it—can be obtained without any cost to their organizations.

Citizenship in a modern democracy involves more than knowledge of how to access vital information. It also involves a capacity to recognize propaganda, distortion, and other misuses and abuses of information. People are daily subjected to statistics about health, the economy, national defense, and countless products. One person arranges the information to prove his point, another arranges it to prove hers. One political party says the social indicators are encouraging, another calls them frightening. One drug company states most doctors prefer its product, another "proves" doctors favor its product. In such an environment, information literacy provides insight into the manifold ways in which people can all be deceived and misled. Information literate citizens are able to spot and expose chicanery, disinformation, and lies.

To say that information literacy is crucial to effective citizenship is simply to say it is central to the practice of democracy. Any society committed to individual freedom and democratic government must ensure the free flow of information to all its citizens in order to protect personal liberties and to guard its future. As U.S. Representative Major R. Owens has said:

Information literacy is needed to guarantee the survival of democratic institutions. All men are created equal but voters with information resources are in a position to make more intelligent decisions than citizens who are information illiterates. The application of information resources to the process of decision-making to fulfill civic responsibilities is a vital necessity.

OPPORTUNITIES TO DEVELOP INFORMATION LITERACY

Information literacy is a survival skill in the Information Age. Instead of drowning in the abundance of information that floods their lives, information literate people know how to find, evaluate, and use information effectively to solve a particular problem or make a decision—whether the information they select comes from a computer, a book, a government agency, a film, or any number of other possible resources. Libraries, which provide a significant public access point to such information and usually at no cost, must play a key role in preparing people for the demands of today's information society. Just as public libraries were once a means of education and a better life for many of the over 20 million immigrants of the late 1800s and early 1900s, they remain today as the potentially strongest and most far-reaching community resource for lifelong learning. Public libraries not only provide access to information, but they also remain crucial to providing people with the knowledge necessary to make meaningful use of existing resources. They remain one of the few safeguards against information control by a minority.

Although libraries historically have provided a meaningful structure for relating information in ways that facilitate the development of knowledge, they have been all but ignored in the literature about the information society. Even national education reform reports, starting with *A Nation at Risk* in 1983, largely exclude libraries. No K–12 report has explored the potential role of libraries or the need for information literacy. In the higher education reform literature, Education Commission of the States President Frank Newman's 1985 report, *Higher Education and the American Resurgence,* only addresses the instructional potential of libraries in passing, but it does raise the concern for the accessibility of materials within the knowledge explosion. In fact, no reform report until *College,* the 1986 Carnegie Foundation Report, gave substantive consideration to the role of libraries in addressing the challenges facing higher education. In the initial release of the study's recommendations, it was noted that

> The quality of a college is measured by the resources for learning on the campus and the extent to which students become independent, self-directed learners. And yet we found that today, about one out of every four undergraduates spends no time in the library during a normal week, and 65 percent use the library four hours or less each week. The gap between the classroom and the library, reported on almost a half-century ago, still exists today.

Statistics such as these document the general passivity of most academic learning today and the divorce of the impact of the Information Age from prevailing teaching styles.

The first step in reducing this gap is making sure that the issue of information literacy is an integral part of current efforts at cultural literacy, the development of critical thinking abilities, and school restructuring. Due to the relative newness of the information society, however, information literacy is often completely overlooked in relevant dialogues, research, and experimentations. Moreover, most current educational and communication endeavors—with their long-standing history of prepackaging information—militate against the development of even an awareness of the need to master information management skills.

The effects of such prepackaging of information are most obvious in the school and academic settings. Students, for example, receive predigested information from lectures and textbooks, and little in their environment fosters active thinking or problem solving. What problem solving does occur is within artificially constructed and limited information environments that allow for single "correct" answers. Such exercises bear little resemblance to problem solving in the real world where multiple solutions of varying degrees of usefulness must be pieced together—often from many disciplines and from multiple information sources such as online databases, videotapes, government documents, and journals.

Education needs a new model of learning—learning that is based on the information resources of the real world and learning that is active and integrated, not passive and fragmented. On an intellectual level, many teachers and school administrators recognize that lectures, textbooks, materials put on reserve, and tests that ask students to regurgitate data from these sources do not create an active, much less a quality, learning experience. Moreover, studies at the higher education level have proven that students fail to retain most information they are "given."

> The curve for forgetting course content is fairly steep: a generous estimate is that students forget 50% of the content within a few months.... A more devastating finding comes from a study that concluded that even under the most favorable conditions, "students carry away in their heads and in their notebook not more than 42% of the lecture content." Those were the results when students were told that they would be tested immediately following the lecture; they were permitted to use their notes; and they were given a prepared summary of the lecture. These results were bad enough, but when students were tested a week later, without the use of their notes, they could recall only 17% of the lecture material.

Because of the rapidly shrinking half-life of information, even the value of that 17 percent that students do remember must be questioned. To any thoughtful person, it must be clear that teaching facts is a poor substitute for teaching people how to learn, i.e., giving them the skills to be able to locate, evaluate, and effectively use information for any given need.

What is called for is not a new information studies curriculum but, rather, a restructuring of the learning process. Textbooks, workbooks, and lectures must yield to a learning process based on the information resources available for learning and problem solving throughout people's lifetimes—to learning experiences that build a lifelong habit of library use. Such a learning process would actively involve students in the process of

- knowing when they have a need for information
- identifying information needed to address a given problem or issue
- finding needed information
- evaluating the information
- organizing the information
- using the information effectively to address the problem or issue at hand.

Such a restructuring of the learning process will not only enhance the critical thinking skills of students but will also empower them for lifelong learning and the effective performance of professional and civic responsibilities.

AN INFORMATION AGE SCHOOL

An increased emphasis on information literacy and resource-based learning would manifest itself in a variety of ways at both the academic and school levels, depending upon the role and mission of the individual institution and the information environment of its community. However, the following description of what a school might be like if information literacy were a central, not a peripheral, concern reveals some of the possibilities. (While focused on K–12, outcomes could be quite similar at the college level.)

The school would be more interactive, because students, pursuing questions of personal interest, would be interacting with other students, with teachers, with a vast array of information resources, and the community at large to a far greater degree than they presently do today. One would expect to find every student engaged in at least one open-ended, long-term quest for an answer to a serious social, scientific, aesthetic, or political problem. Students' quests would involve not only searching print, electronic, and video data, but also interviewing people inside and outside of school. As a result, learning would be more self-initiated. There would be more reading of original sources and more extended writing. Both students and teachers would be familiar with the intellectual and emotional demands of asking productive questions, gathering data of all kinds, reducing and synthesizing information, and analyzing, interpreting, and evaluating information in all its forms.

In such an environment, teachers would be coaching and guiding students more and lecturing less. They would have long since discovered that the classroom computer, with its access to the libraries and databases of the world, is a better source of facts than they could ever hope to be. They would have come to see that their major importance lies in their capacity to arouse curiosity and guide it to a satisfactory conclusion, to ask the right questions at the right time, to stir debate and serious discussion, and to be models themselves of thoughtful inquiry.

Teachers would work consistently with librarians, media resource people, and instructional designers both within their schools and in their communities to ensure that student projects and explorations are challenging, interesting, and productive learning experiences in which they can all take pride. It would not be surprising in such a school to find a student task force exploring an important community issue with a view toward making a public presentation of its findings on cable television or at a news conference. Nor would it be unusual to see the librarian guiding the task force through its initial questions and its multidisciplinary, multimedia search—all the way through to its cable or satellite presentation. In such a role, librarians would be valued for their information expertise and their technological know-how. They would lead frequent in-service teacher workshops and ensure that the school was getting the most out of its investment in information technology.

Because evaluation in such a school would also be far more interactive than it is today, it would also be a much better learning experience. Interactive tutoring software that guides students through their own and other knowledge bases would provide more useful diagnostic information than is available today. Evaluation would be based upon a broad range of literacy indicators, including some that assess the quality and appropriateness of information sources or the quality and efficiency of the information searches themselves. Assessments would attend to ways in which students are using their minds and achieving success as information consumers, analyzers, interpreters, evaluators, and communicators of ideas.

Finally, one would expect such a school to look and sound different from today's schools. One would see more information technology than is evident today, and it would be important to people not only in itself but also in regard to its capacity to help them solve problems and create knowledge. One would see the fruits of many student projects prominently displayed on the walls and on bookshelves, and one would hear more discussions and debate about substantive, relevant issues. On the playground, in the halls, in the cafeteria, and certainly in the classroom, one would hear fundamental questions that make information literacy so important: "How do you know that?" and "What evidence do you have for that?" "Who says?" and "How can we find out?"

CONCLUSION

This call for more attention to information literacy comes at a time when many other learning deficiencies are being expressed by educators, business leaders, and parents. Many workers, for example, appear unprepared to deal effectively with the challenges of high-tech equipment. There exists a need for better thinkers, problem solvers, and inquirers. There are calls for computer literacy, civic literacy, global literacy, and cultural literacy. Because we have been hit by a tidal wave of information, what used to suffice as literacy no longer suffices; what used to count as effective knowledge no longer meets our needs; what used to pass as a good education no longer is adequate.

The one common ingredient in all of these concerns is an awareness of the rapidly changing requirements for a productive, healthy, and satisfying life. To respond effectively to an ever-changing environment, people need more than just a knowledge base, they also need techniques for exploring it, connecting it to other knowledge bases, and making practical use of it. In other words, the landscape upon which we used to stand has been transformed, and we are being forced to establish a new foundation called information literacy. Now knowledge—not minerals or agricultural products or manufactured goods—is this country's most precious commodity, and people who are information literate—who know how to acquire knowledge and use it—are America's most valuable resource.

COMMITTEE RECOMMENDATIONS

To reap the benefits from the Information Age by our country, its citizens, and its businesses, the American Library Association Presidential Committee on Information Literacy makes the following recommendations:

1. *We all must reconsider the ways we have organized information institutionally, structured information access, and defined information's role in our lives at home, in the community, and in the work place.* To the extent that our concepts about knowledge and information are out of touch with the realities of a new, dynamic information environment, we must reconceptualize them. The degrees and directions of reconceptualization will vary, but the aims should always be the same: to communicate the power of knowledge; to develop in each citizen a sense of his or her responsibility to acquire knowledge and deepen insight through better use of information and related technologies; to instill a love of learning, a thrill in searching, and a joy in discovering; and to teach young and old alike how to know when they have an information need and how to gather, synthesize, analyze, interpret, and evaluate the information around them. All of these abilities are equally important for the enhancement of life experiences and for business pursuits.

Colleges, schools, and businesses should pay special attention to the potential role of their libraries or information centers. These should be central, not peripheral; organizational redesigns should seek to empower students and adults through new kinds of access to information and new ways of creating, discovering, and sharing it.

2. *A Coalition for Information Literacy should be formed under the leadership of the American Library Association, in coordination with other national organizations and agencies, to promote information literacy.* The major obstacle to promoting information literacy is a lack of public awareness of the problems created by information illiteracy. The need for increased information literacy levels in all aspects of people's lives—in business, in family matters, and civic responsibilities—must be brought to the public's attention in a forceful way. To accomplish this, the Coalition should serve as an educational network for communications, coalescing related educational efforts, developing leadership, and effecting change. The Coalition should monitor and report on state efforts to promote information literacy and resource-based learning and provide recognition of individuals and programs for their exemplary information literacy efforts.

The Coalition should be organized with an advisory committee made up of nationally prominent public figures from librarianship, education, business, and government. The responsibilities of the advisory committee should include support for Coalition efforts in the areas of capturing media attention, raising public awareness, and fostering a climate favorable for information literacy. In addition, the advisory committee should actively seek funding to promote research and demonstration projects.

3. *Research and demonstration projects related to information and its use need to be undertaken.* To date, remarkably little research has been done to understand how information can be more effectively managed to meet educational and societal objectives or to explore how information management skills impact on overall school and academic performance. What research does exist appears primarily in library literature, which is seldom read by educators or state decision makers.

For future efforts to be successful, a national research agenda should be developed and implemented. The number of issues needing to be addressed are significant and should include the following:

- What are the social effects of reading?
- With electronic media eclipsing reading for many people, what will be the new place of the printed word?

- How do the characteristics of information resources (format, length, age) affect their usefulness?
- How does the use of information vary by discipline?
- How does access to information impact on the effectiveness of citizen action groups?
- How do information management skills affect student performance and retention?
- What role can information management skills play in the economic and social advancement of minorities?

Also needed is research that will promote a "sophisticated understanding of the full range of the issues and processes related to the generation, distribution, and use of information so that libraries can fulfill their obligations to their users and potential users and so that research and scholarship in all fields can flourish."

The Coalition can play a major role in obtaining funding for such research and for fostering demonstration projects that can provide fertile ground for controlled experiments that can contrast benefits from traditional versus resource-based learning opportunities for students.

4. *State Departments of Education, Commissions on Higher Education, and Academic Governing Boards should be responsible to ensure that a climate conducive to students' becoming information literate exists in their states and on their campuses.* Of importance are two complementary issues: the development of an information literate citizenry and the move from textbook and lecture-style learning to resource-based learning. The latter is, in fact, the means to the former as well as to producing lifelong, independent, and self-directed learners. As is appropriate within their stated missions, such bodies are urged to do the following:

- To incorporate the spirit and intent of information literacy into curricular requirements, recommendations, and instructional materials. (Two excellent models for state school guidelines are Washington's "Information Skills Curriculum Guide: Process Scope and Sequence" and "Library Information Skills: Guide for Oregon Schools K-12.")
- To incorporate in professional preparation and in-service training for teachers an appreciation for the importance of resource-based learning, to encourage implementation of it in their subject areas, and to provide opportunities to master implementation techniques.
- To encourage and support coordination of school/campus and public library resources/services with classroom instruction in offering resource-based learning.

- To include coverage of information literacy competencies in state assessment examinations.
- To establish recognition programs of exemplary projects for learning information management skills in elementary and secondary schools, in higher education institutions, and in professional preparation programs.

5. *Teacher education and performance expectations should be modified to include information literacy concerns.* Inherent in the concepts of information literacy and resource-based learning is the complementary concept of the teacher as a facilitator of student learning rather than as presenter of ready-made information. To be successful in such roles, teachers should make use of an expansive array of information resources. They should be familiar with and able to use selected databases, learning networks, reference materials, textbooks, journals, newspapers, magazines, and other resources. They also should place a premium on problem solving and see that their classrooms are extended outward to encompass the learning resources of the library media centers and the community. They also should expect their students to become information literate.

To encourage the development of teachers who are facilitators of learning, the following recommendations are made to schools of teacher education. Those responsible for in-service teacher training should also evaluate current capabilities of teaching professionals and incorporate the following recommendations into their programs as needed.

- New knowledge from cognitive research on thinking skills should be incorporated into pedagogical skills development.
- Integral to all programs should be instruction in managing the classroom, individualizing instruction, setting problems, questioning, promoting cooperative learning—all of which should rely on case studies and information resources of the entire school and community.
- Instruction within the disciplines needs to emphasize a problem-solving approach and the development of a sophisticated level of information management skills appropriate to the individual disciplines.
- School library media specialists need to view the instructional goals of their schools as an integral part of their own concern and responsibilities and should actively contribute toward the ongoing professional development of teachers and principals. They should be members of curriculum and instructional teams and provide leadership in integrating appropriate information and educational technologies into

school programming. (For further recommendations regarding the role of library media specialists, consult *Information Power: Guidelines for School Media Programs* prepared by the American Association of School Librarians and the Association for Educational Communications and Technology, 1988.)

- Exit requirements from teacher education programs should include each candidate's ability to use selected databases, networks, reference materials, administrative and instructional software packages, and new forms of learning technologies.
- A portion of the practicum or teaching experience of beginning teachers should be spent with library media specialists. These opportunities should be based in the school library media center to promote an understanding of resources available in both that facility and other community libraries and to emphasize the concepts and skills necessary to become a learning facilitator.
- Cooperative, or supervising, teachers who can demonstrate their commitment to thinking skills instruction and information literacy should be matched with student teachers, and teachers who see themselves as learning facilitators should be relied upon to serve as role models. Student teachers should also have the opportunity to observe and practice with a variety of models for the teaching of critical thinking.

6. *An understanding of the relationship of information literacy to the themes of the White House Conference on Library and Information Services should be promoted.* The White House conference themes of literacy, productivity, and democracy will provide a unique opportunity to foster public awareness of the importance of information literacy. The American Library Association and the Coalition on Information Literacy should aggressively promote consideration of information literacy within state deliberations as well as within the White House conference itself.

BACKGROUND TO REPORT

The American Library Association's Presidential Committee on Information Literacy was appointed in 1987 by ALA President Margaret Chisholm with three expressed purposes: (1) to define information literacy within the higher literacies and its importance to student performance, lifelong learning, and active citizenship; (2) to design one or more models for information literacy development appropriate to formal and informal learning environments throughout people's lifetimes; and (3) to determine implications for the continuing education and development of teachers. The

Committee, which consists of leaders in education and librarianship, has worked actively to accomplish its mission since its establishment. Members of the Committee include the following:

Gordon M. Ambach, Executive Director
Council of Chief State School Officers

William L. Bainbridge, President
SchoolMatch

Patricia Senn Breivik, Chair, Director
Auraria Library, University of Colorado at Denver

Rexford Brown, Director
Policies and the Higher Literacies Project
Education Commission of the States

Judith S. Eaton, President
Community College of Philadelphia

David Imig, Executive Director
American Association of Colleges for Teacher Education

Sally Kilgore, Professor
Emory University
(former Director of the Office of Research, U.S. Department of Education)

Carol Kuhlthau, Director
Educational Media Services Programs
Rutgers University

Joseph Mika, Director
Library Science Program
Wayne State University

Richard D. Miller, Executive Director
American Association of School Administrators

Roy D. Miller, Executive Assistant to the Director
Brooklyn Public Library

Sharon J. Rogers, University Librarian
George Washington University

Robert Wedgeworth, Dean
School of Library Service
Columbia University

THIS REPORT WAS RELEASED ON JANUARY 10, 1989, IN WASHINGTON, DC

Further Information

Further information on information literacy can be obtained by contacting:

Information Literacy and K–12
   c/o American Association of School Librarians
   American Library Association
   50 East Huron Street
   Chicago, IL 60611

Information Literacy and Higher Education
   c/o Association of College and Research Libraries
   American Library Association
   50 East Huron Street
   Chicago, IL 60611

APPENDIX B

WASHINGTON STATE INFORMATION SKILLS CURRICULUM SCOPE AND SEQUENCE K-12

This publication was printed with permission from the Office of Superintendent of Public Instruction, Olympia, Washington.

The code used on the grids on pages 170–177 represents the suggested levels at which skills may be introduced, expanded, mastered, and reinforced. As you use this scope and sequence, you may wish to adjust these grade levels to fit your own program.

SCOPE AND SEQUENCE K-12

PRE-SEARCH STEPS	BLOOM'S TAXONOMY	K	1	2	3	4	5	6	7	8	9	10	11	12
The student will be able to....														
I: FORMULATE THE CENTRAL QUESTION														
A. Identify the purpose of the research by focusing on a specific question to be answered.	Knowledge		I	E				M	R					
B. Use a variety of questioning skills (yes/no, open ended, probing).	Application				I	E				M	R			
C. Formulate the central question/thesis statement.	Synthesis						I				M	R		
II: RELATE QUESTION TO PRIOR KNOWLEDGE														
A. Brainstorm ideas and information about the central question by recalling previous personal/learning experiences.	Knowledge		I	E			M	R						
B. Locate, identify, and use broad, general information resources.														
1. Use information from the general resource materials to identify major/significant sources of information regarding the central question.	Knowledge Application													
2. Recall words, terms, methods, facts, concepts, specific items, by using broad, general information resources.	Knowledge													
C. Relate all prior knowledge to the central question or thesis.	Application			I	E				M	R				
III: IDENTIFY KEY WORDS AND NAMES														
A. Understand the purpose of compiling bits and pieces of information for later use.	Comprehension													
1. Identify key words and phrases.	Knowledge			I	E				M	R				
2. Locate major headings/groupings.	Knowledge													

KEY: I-Introduce. E-Expand. M-Mastery. R-Reinforce

SCOPE AND SEQUENCE K-12

	BLOOM'S TAXONOMY	K	1	2	3	4	5	6	7	8	9	10	11	12
3. Skim or scan for major ideas.	Knowledge				I ——	E ——	——	——	M ——	R				
B. Identify key words. 1. Use context clues for key word identification. 2. Understand the definitions of key words related to the central question. 3. Use personal knowledge and general resource materials to list all key words, phrases, subtopic headings, major headings/groupings which could be used to search the central question.	Knowledge Application Comprehension Application				I ——	E ——	——	——	——	M ——	R			
C. Identify the library subject headings and database descriptors which relate to the central question or thesis.	Knowledge							I ——	——	——	——	——	M ——	R	
IV. INTEGRATE CONCEPTS														
A. Recognize a variety of ways to organize material in order to clarify relationships among terms and ideas. (lists, clustering, webbing, etc.)	Knowledge				I ——	E ——	——	——	——	——	M ——	R		
B. Demonstrate the ability to create one or more of the following: -list -cluster -traditional outline -mind map -radial outline	Comprehension		I ——	——	E ——	——	——	——	E ——	M ——	R			
C. Incorporate key words and phrases into an appropriate method of organization.	Application				I ——	E ——	——	——	——	M ——	R			
D. Restate phrases/concepts in individual's own words.	Comprehension				I ——	E ——	——	——	E ——	——	——	M ——	R	
E. Inspect the method of organization to determine missing elements.	Analysis							I ——	——	E ——	——	——	M ——	R	

SCOPE AND SEQUENCE K-12

	BLOOM'S TAXONOMY	K	1	2	3	4	5	6	7	8	9	10	11	12
V: DEVELOP QUESTIONS TO ORGANIZE SEARCH														
A. Summarize the main ideas regarding the central question.	Comprehension	I	E								M	R		
B. Express the ideas in a simple sentence form.	Comprehension			I	E					M	R			
C. Ask questions to clarify meaning.	Comprehension	I	E							M	R			
D. Construct questions about the central question, based on the method of organization.	Synthesis					I	E			M	R			
E. Discriminate between important and less important questions, and exclude the least important questions.	Evaluation					I	E			M	R			
F. Create a plan for the search based on the resulting questions by refining the working outline as important information is discovered.	Synthesis					I	E			M	R			
VI: (WHEN NEEDED) RE-EXPLORE GENERAL RESOURCES														
A. Re-examine the general resource materials used in Step #3.	Synthesis					I	E			M	R			
B. Revise the central question or thesis statement if necessary.	Synthesis					I	E					M	R	
C. Redefine the central question or thesis statement if necessary.	Synthesis					I	E			M	R			

KEY: I-Introduce. E-Expand. M-Mastery. R-Reinforce

SCOPE AND SEQUENCE K-12

THE SEARCH

VII: LOCATE RESOURCES OF INFORMATION

	Bloom's Taxonomy	K	1	2	3	4	5	6	7	8	9	10	11	12
A. Recognize and use the library media center resources, including the consulting role of the library media specialist.	Knowledge		I				E					M		
B. Reconsider general resource materials located in Steps II and III. Examine other resources such as periodicals, newspapers, special encyclopedias, non-print materials, etc.	Comprehension/ Knowledge				I	E						M	R	
C. Consider resources outside of the school library media center: public library, community, home, experts, on-line computer searches, etc.	Knowledge				I	E						M		
D. Demonstrate library media center location skills.														
1. Recognize that library materials are indexed, and that this index may be in a variety of forms (card catalog, microfiche, on-line computer, etc.)	Application Comprehension		I I									M M	R R	
2. Recognize that all indexes (card catalog, Reader's Guide, ERIC, etc.) are in alphabetical order.	Comprehension			I	E				M	R				
3. Identify author, title, and subject entries.	Knowledge		I	E	E		M	R						
4. Locate basic essential information on any given index entry.	Knowledge			I	E			M	R					
5. Use subject headings and cross references to find additional resources.	Application							I	E			M	R	
E. Locate and select the most useful sources from among those available.	Knowledge/ Analysis				I	E				M	R			

VIII. SEARCH FOR RELEVANT INFORMATION

	Bloom's Taxonomy	K	1	2	3	4	5	6	7	8	9	10	11	12
A. Locate the sections of the resource that are useful in answering the search questions generated in Step V.	Knowledge				I	E				M	R			
B. Skim the article or media to find a word, name, date, phrase, idea, or general overview of the resource.	Comprehension				I	E				M	R			

KEY: I-Introduce. E-Expand. M-Mastery. R-Reinforce

SCOPE AND SEQUENCE K-12

	BLOOM'S TAXONOMY	K	1	2	3	4	5	6	7	8	9	10	11	12
C. Find and make effective use of the relevant sections in time-based media, such as videotapes and films.	Knowledge/ Application					I	E		R					
D. Continue to build on compiling skills, as introduced in Step III. 1. Determine gaps in information collected. 2. Determine if additional sources are needed.	Comprehension					I	E		R					
E. Compile bibliographic information for each resource. 1. Define and explain the purpose of a bibliography. 2. Identify the essential parts of a bibliographic entry (author, title, copyright date, publisher, medium, etc.)	Synthesis Knowledge Knowledge					I	E				M	R		
F. Access relevant records through searching a computer database. 1. Understand the concept of a database, and specifically an on-line database. 2. Determine the possible databases to be searched. 3. Design the search strategy, narrowing the search parameters as needed.	Application Comprehension Comprehension Synthesis							I	E			M	R	
G. Continue to conduct primary research as needed. 1. Plan for and complete an interview. 2. Plan and conduct a survey/questionnaire. 3. Write a letter of inquiry.	Application Synthesis Synthesis Knowledge							I	E			M	R	

INTERPRETATION

IX: SELECT AND EVALUATE INFORMATION

		K	1	2	3	4	5	6	7	8	9	10	11	12
A. Evaluate for currency of information. 1. Identify copyright date. 2. Understand the significance of dated vs current information.	Evaluation Knowledge Knowledge				I	E			M	R				

KEY: I-Introduce. E-Expand. M-Mastery. R-Reinforce

SCOPE AND SEQUENCE K-12

		BLOOM'S TAXONOMY	K	1	2	3	4	5	6	7	8	9	10	11	12
B.	Identify the contributor/producer of the sources being used.	Knowledge					I	E			M	R			
C.	Evaluate the contributor's/producer's work for motive, point of view, bias, authority, intended audience, etc.	Evaluation								I	E		M	R	
D.	Distinguish among fact, nonfact, opinion and propaganda.	Evaluation					I	E				M	R		
E.	Select information that is most useful in meeting the needs of the central question (Step V). Eliminate irrelevant information.	Analysis					I	E				M	R		

X. INTERPRET, INFER, ANALYZE, AND PARAPHRASE

A.	Read, view or listen to sources, identifying main ideas, opinions and supporting facts.	Knowledge/ Comprehension			I	E							M	R		
B.	Summarize and paraphrase important facts and details that support the central question (Step V). Compile notes/information according to the working outline developed in Step V.	Evaluation					I	E				M	R		
C.	Interpret graphic sources for information: maps, charts, pictures, diagrams, bar and picture graphs, tables, etc.	Evaluation					I	E		E		M	R		
D.	Derive valid inferences from information sources.	Evaluation					I	E				M	R		

APPLICATION

XI: ORGANIZE INFORMATION FOR APPLICATIONS

A.	Compare, summarize and generalize information from all sources.	Evaluation					I	E			M	R			

KEY: I-Introduce. E-Expand. M-Mastery. R-Reinforce

175

SCOPE AND SEQUENCE K-12

	BLOOM'S TAXONOMY	K	1	2	3	4	5	6	7	8	9	10	11	12
B. Select an appropriate organizational style. Possible methods would include: 1. Chronological 2. Three-step action a. Give an example, relevant to the subject, based on personal experience. b. Explain the action or belief which you propose/hold. c. Give either a reason for or the benefit derived from the action. 3. Argumenative position 4. Order of importance 5. Space order 6. Problem - Solution 7. Topical	Analysis								I	E		M	R	
C. Determine the most effective method of presentation for the selected organizational style. In order to make this decision the student must be given guidance in the following skills: 1. Identification and operation of a variety of media equipment. (Filmstrip projector, audio cassette recorder, video cassette recorder, video camera. 2. Pracice in presenting thoughts, feelings, and creative ideas through student produced media: books, posters, transparencies, slide shows, puppets, audio and video tapes, etc.)	Comprehension Knowledge Comprehension	I	E						M	R				
D. Plan the project (written paper, oral presentation, slide show, videotape, demonstration, exhibit, etc.) using the selected organizational style. 1. Decide on purpose: to inform, persuade, entertain. 2. Determine main points to be made or arguments to be developed and adapt working outline. 3. Use the composition process; including prewriting, rough draft, writing/designing/scripting, etc. 4. Prepare a bibliography if appropriae and/or required for the presentation.	Synthesis Analysis Analysis Application Application				I	E						M	R	

KEY: I-Introduce. E-Expand. M-Mastery. R-Reinforce

SCOPE AND SEQUENCE K-12

	BLOOM'S TAXONOMY	K	1	2	3	4	5	6	7	8	9	10	11	12
XII: APPLY INFORMATION FOR INTENDED PURPOSE														
A. Make a clear, well-supported presentation which answers the central question; or solve the problem by applying search information.	Synthesis				I――E							――M	R―	
B. Draw conclusions based on search information.	Evaluation						I―	―E―	――M	R―				
C. Evaluate the project and the search process.	Evaluation						I―	―E―	――M	R―				

KEY: I-Introduce. E-Expand. M-Mastery. R-Reinforce

For information about receiving a copy of the complete curriculum guide, write to: Superintendent of Public Instruction, Old Capitol Building, P.O. Box 47200, Olympia, WA 98504-7200.

APPENDIX C

NATIONAL EDUCATION GOALS AND THE FOUR STRATEGY TRACKS IDENTIFIED IN AMERICA 2000: AN EDUCATION STRATEGY

NATIONAL EDUCATION GOALS

By the year 2000:

1. All children in America will start school ready to learn.
2. The high school graduation rate will increase to at least 90 percent.
3. American students will leaves grades four, eight, and twelve having demonstrated competency in challenging subject matter including English, mathematics, science, history, and geography; and every school in America will ensure that all students learn to use their minds well, so they may be prepared for responsible citizenship, further learning, and productive employment in our modern economy.
4. U.S. students will be first in the world in science and mathematics achievement.
5. Every adult American will be literate and will possess the knowledge and skills necessary to compete in a global economy and exercise the rights and responsibilities of citizenship.
6. Every school in America will be free of drugs and violence and will offer a disciplined environment conducive to learning.

THE FOUR STRATEGY TRACKS IDENTIFIED IN *AMERICA 2000: AN EDUCATION STRATEGY*

For today's students, we must radically improve today's schools by making all 110,000 of them better and more accountable for results.

For tomorrow's students, we must invent new schools to meet the demands of a new century with a New Generation of American Schools, bringing at least 535 of them into existence by 1996 and thousands by decade's end.

For those of us already out of school and in the workforce, we must keep learning if we are to live and work successfully in today's world. A "Nation at Risk" must become a "Nation of Students."

For schools to succeed, we must look beyond our classrooms to our communities and families. Schools will never be much better than the commitment of their communities. Each of our communities must become a place where learning can happen.

APPENDIX D
NATIONAL FORUM ON INFORMATION LITERACY MEMBERSHIP LIST

ABC News Interactive
American Association for Adult Continuing Education
American Association of Colleges for Teacher Education
American Association of Community Colleges
American Association for Higher Education
American Association of School Administrators
American Association of School Librarians
American Association of University Professors
American Library Association
American Society for Public Administration
Association of American Publishers
Association of College and Research Libraries
Association for Educational Communications and Technology
Association for Library and Information Science Education
Association of Public Data Users
Association for Supervision and Curriculum Development
Center for Law and Education, Inc.
Chief Officers of State Library Agencies
College Board
Commission on Higher Education Middle States Associations
Council of Chief State School Officers
Council of Independent Colleges
Education Commission of the States
EDUCOM
EPIE Institute
ERIC Clearinghouse on Information Resources
Friends of Libraries U.S.A.
Hispanic Policy Development Project
Information Industry Association
International Visual Literacy Association
Newspaper Association of America Foundation
National Alliance of Black School Educators
National Association of Counties
National Association of Partners in Education
National Association of Secondary School Principals
National Association of State Boards of Education
National Association of State Directors of Vocational Education
National Community Education Association
National Commission on Libraries & Information Science
National Conference of State Legislatures
National Consumers League
National Coordinating Committee for the Promotion of History
National Council for the Social Studies
National Council of Teachers of English
National Council of Teachers of Mathematics
National Education Association
National Forum for Black Public Administrators
National Forum on Information Literacy
National Governors' Association
National Partners for Libraries and Literacy
National School Boards Association
National Science Teachers Association
Office of Educational Research and Improvement U. S. Department of Education
People For the American Way
Project Censored
Special Libraries Association
State Higher Education Executive Offices
U.S. Small Business Administration
Women in Communications, Inc.

APPENDIX E

CHRISTINA S. DOYLE'S 1992 EXECUTIVE SUMMARY AS IT RELATES TO THE NATIONAL EDUCATION GOAL III

Goal III has a critical focus on students learning to use their minds well—knowing how to learn in order to make informed decisions. During the years of general education (K–12), all students need to learn how to process information as they apply problem solving and critical thinking skills regularly in school and personal areas. To learn these skills requires an active learning format where students process information to meet specific needs at a level that is developmentally appropriate. The inquiry approach is basic to active learning. An information-rich environment is needed, with many resources available, including computer-based and other technologies. Teachers will need skills to facilitate resource-based learning.

Comments by the panel members supported the concept that teachers are the most critical key to student attainment of information literacy. Because active learning represents a major shift in instructional strategies, shift not often addressed in teacher preparation, massive staff development must be conducted. It needs to be ongoing over a period of years as teachers build confidence and develop applications for their own classes. They must become information literate themselves, comfortable with the variety of resources as well as the process of accessing, evaluating, and using information. Furthermore, assessments that integrate the process of information literacy into meaningful final projects, portfolios, or performances must be developed.

A library/media center stocked with a wide variety of print-nonprint resources was identified as critical to the implementation of information literacy. Staffed with a trained library/media specialist who collaborates with classroom teachers to carry out classroom objectives, the library/media center becomes the hub of a school. Equity of access to resources increases.

Resource sharing between school and community was mentioned frequently, a recognition that rising costs and evolving technologies call for rethinking traditional institutions. The point was well made that reference to no/low cost resources was misleading. There are always costs to accessing information. It must be determined at what point payment will be made. This research points to equity of access being guaranteed at the highest possible level (federal, state), rather than penalizing those who cannot pay for opportunities to be knowledgeable.

Implications are that in order for students to become self-motivated, policy must facilitate the following:

- National/state governments must make a commitment to ensure that all students have equal and regular access to information by assuring adequate resources at each site.
- State Departments of Education/local school systems will develop and implement a resource-based learning curriculum.
- Curriculum standards that reflect a resource-based learning approach will be developed.
- Ongoing in-services will be conducted to ensure that teachers have the skills necessary to facilitate resource-based learning.
- Library/media centers will be recognized as key to successful implementation of resource-based learning.
- Parental support and participation in their children's learning will be considered integral.
- School goals will assure that information literacy skills are included across all curricular areas, so that all students apply information literacy as they learn the underlying principles of each curricular area.
- Sites will develop curricular objectives that include the process of information literacy across all curricular disciplines in the context of basic principles that are inherent to a particular subject area.
- Sites will develop curricular assessment methods that include alternative assessment procedures such as projects, portfolios, and performances and integrate the information literacy process.
- The library/media specialist will be an integral part of the instructional program, working in coordination with classroom teachers to carry out the curricular objectives.
- Teachers will implement resource-based learning in their classrooms.
- A variety of teaching strategies will be used to support students as active learners.
- Critical thinking/problem-solving skills will be developed and honed through meaningful activities involving the location and interpretation of information.
- Ongoing demonstrations will be made of how facts learned in classes become woven together to reveal the interrelated patterns of the world.
- Student assessment procedures will be used that include demonstration of the information literacy process, as through portfolios, projects, and performances.
- The library/media center will be viewed as an extension of the classroom.

Given, then, the close relationship of information literacy to the accomplishment of key National Education Goals and the demands of the workforce, the promotion of resource-based learning, as a practical means to produce information literate citizens and workers, would seem a wise endeavor on the part of the principals.

APPENDIX F

IMPLEMENTING THE COLORADO STATE BOARD OF EDUCATION GOALS THROUGH SCHOOL LIBRARY MEDIA PROGRAMS

GRADUATION RATE

Colorado's statewide public school graduation rate will increase by two percent annually from the 1987 rate of 76 percent until it reaches at least 90 percent by July 1, 1995.

All Colorado schools will have established procedures in grades K-3 to identify potential at-risk students and provide them with successful learning experiences upon identification.

All Colorado schools will have educational programs in place that adequately prepare all students to enter and succeed in their next level of enrollment. These programs will provide students with appropriate skills and will ensure their continuous progress toward graduation from high school.

Major contributions: As instructional consultants, library media specialists work with classroom teachers in matching instructional materials to students' learning needs and styles. The school library media center serves as an extension of the classroom, a learning laboratory, where all students have access to multimedia materials at various learning levels.

STUDENT ACHIEVEMENT

Colorado's public school system will have demonstrated continuous, measurable, and significant gains in educational achievement for all student groups by July 1, 1995.

By July 1, 1991, Colorado's school districts will have defined their expected student proficiencies at designated grade levels, and will have implemented a program of measurement and reporting.

By July 1, 1995, all Colorado high school graduates will receive a diploma certifying that they possess the skills deemed by the local board of education to be necessary for entry to the work place and post-secondary education.

Major Contributions: Library media specialists, working as information specialists, teachers, and instructional consultants, help students develop lifelong learning skills, thinking skills, and the ability to use information effectively.

Examples:
1. Through the library media program, students are encouraged to use multiple sources and types of media to locate, select, evaluate, organize, and present information.
2. Library media specialists, working with classroom teachers, design curriculum that helps students develop thinking and problem solving skills.
3. The integration of information skills into the curriculum enables students to become independent, self-directed learners.
4. The library media center collection contains a wide variety of current materials for varying abilities and student learning styles.
5. The library media specialist, working in a partnership with classroom teachers, works in developing alternative assessments to encourage students to use multimedia in demonstrating proficiencies.
6. The use of technology motivates many students and enhances student achievement.
7. The media center encourages and supports interdisciplinary learning.
8. A library media center which is open and staffed before and after school, during student lunch hours, and throughout the school day offers strong support for student achievement.
9. Student achievement can be highlighted through displays in the library media center.
10. Materials in the library media center reflect many cultures, places, times, and points of view.
11. Current resources are available for students to explore global issues and multicultural concerns.
12. Through resource sharing and networking, students can obtain information from other libraries throughout the country.
13. Use of databases, online searching, and distance learning can give students additional current information.
14. The library media center provides instruction for entire classes, small groups, and individuals.
15. The library media specialist can develop information skills outcomes and proficiencies for integration within content areas.

Examples:
1. The use of multimedia materials and a variety of technologies in addition to print formats can help all students achieve success.

2. The library media center offers a non-competitive climate which gives students an opportunity to be successful.
3. Students' preferred learning styles can be accommodated by materials available in a wide range of formats and difficulty levels in the library media center's collection.
4. Library media specialists frequently work with individual students or small groups of students in cooperative learning situations. Individualized support encourages all students, particularly those who are at-risk.
5. Students are motivated to learn using technology. Technology often provides an excellent learning tool for the at-risk student.
6. The learning of information skills, as integrated with the curriculum, enables students to access, evaluate, and use information and become independent, self-directed learners.
7. The library media specialist works collaboratively with classroom teachers to develop and implement curriculum using a wide variety of materials and approaches to meet students' learning needs.
8. The media center can highlight student achievement in a variety of areas through displays, bulletin boards, etc.
9. Popular materials to meet student interests are provided.
10. Career explorations and materials are available in the library media center.
11. The library media center collection reflects the diversity of our multicultural society.
12. Materials in languages other than English meet the learning needs of special populations.

APPENDIX G

HIGHLIGHTS FROM THE IMPACT OF SCHOOL LIBRARY MEDIA CENTERS ON ACADEMIC ACHIEVEMENTS

from the Colorado Department of Education,
201 E. Colfax, Denver, CO 80203

This publication was printed with permission from the Colorado Department of Education, Denver, CO.

THE IMPACT OF SCHOOL LIBRARY MEDIA CENTERS ON ACADEMIC ACHIEVEMENT

Keith Curry Lance
Lynda Welborn
Christine Hamilton-Pennell

William T. Randall
Commissioner of Education

Nancy M. Bolt
*Assistant Commissioner
State Library & Adult Education Office*

Colorado Department of Education
201 E. Colfax
Denver, CO 80203

Prepared for the U.S. Department of Education
Office of Educational Research & Improvement Library Programs
September 1992

This research was supported by a $69,664
Library Research & Demonstration Grant No. R039A00008-90.

CHAPTER 1
INTRODUCTION

School library media advocates need evidence of the links between quality library media centers (LMCs) and academic achievement. This need was demonstrated by the unprecedented publicity surrounding 1987-88 reports of a proprietary study which correlated library media expenditures and scores on norm-referenced tests.[1] Remarkably, few studies have been published on the subject over the past thirty years, and, for the most part, they only support establishing library media centers and library media specialist (LMS) positions, not strengthening them.

This study was designed to develop better empirical evidence of the impact of school library media centers on academic achievement in Colorado's public schools. It will also facilitate the development of such evidence in other states.

This first chapter identifies questions about the impact of LMCs on academic achievement for which answers will be sought, reviews previous studies on the topic, and outlines the balance of this report.

1.1 Questions About the Impact of School Library Media Centers on Academic Achievement

Answers to three specific questions will be sought by this study:

- Is there, in fact, a relationship between expenditures on LMCs and test performance, particularly when economic differences between communities and schools are controlled? Do test scores rise and fall with the fiscal fate of library media programs?

- Assuming such a relationship, what characteristics of library media programs intervene to help to explain the relationship between expenditures on them, and norm-referenced test scores? Can the number and level of LMC staff or the number of items or variety of formats in the collection be linked to test performance?

- Does the performance of an instructional role by library media specialists help to predict norm-referenced test scores? Does the amount of collaboration between library media specialists and their colleagues in the classroom affect test performance?

In pursuing answers to these three questions, this study was designed to identify schools rather than students as units of analysis, use service outputs as well as resource inputs as measures of quality, and rule out school and community differences which might explain away important relationships between LMCs and academic achievement.

This design will permit the use of readily available, aggregate data for a large number of schools statewide. It will also permit the application of rigorous statistical techniques to assess the relative importance of the many predictors

---

[1] American Library Association, "Pupil success firmly linked to school library funding," *American Libraries* 18:8 (September 1987), 632-33; Lynch, Mary Jo and Weeks, Ann, "School Match revisited," *American Libraries* 19:6 (June 1988), 459-60.

under consideration. Thus, rather than simply comparing test performance by the library media "haves" and "have nots," this study will attempt to measure the impact of incremental differences in library media programs.

1.2 Review of the Literature

During the past thirty years, fewer than 40 research studies have focused on the impact of school library media centers on academic achievement. The majority of those studies (27) occurred between 1959 and 1979. Obviously, the quantitative research in this field is limited. In addition, these studies are limited in scope. Generally, a small number of subjects in a limited geographical area were examined. Often, these studies focused on one city or, at the most, a state (the exception being Gaver (1963), who looked at data from 13 states). The span of the studies was for a limited time period, generally no more than a few months. The only longitudinal study was completed by Thorne (1967) in a two-year study of students involved in the Knapp School Libraries Project. Neither of these limitations will be remedied by the design of this study. However, the study contributes several new elements to the overall field of research.

1.2.1 Presence of Library Media Center

Early studies (Willson, 1965; Yarling, 1968; Ainsworth, 1969; Becker, 1970; McConnaha, 1972) dealt with the value of the mere presence of a library, reflecting the prevalence of classroom collections and the lack of centralized library service, particularly at the elementary level.

- Wilson (1965) showed that students demonstrated superior gains on the Iowa Test of Basic Skills (ITBS) in elementary schools with a centralized library and a professional librarian.

- Yarling (1968) found that the addition of a well-equipped and managed centralized library had a significant impact on the performance of elementary school students in library-related skills, particularly outlining and notetaking.

- Students who used a new fully staffed and equipped elementary school library showed significant improvement in library skills test scores in the study by Ainsworth (1969).

- Becker (1970) compared ITBS scores between students in elementary schools with and without libraries and found that the presence of a library and the guidance and function of a librarian appeared to exert significant influence on pupil achievement in some information-gathering skills areas.

- McConnaha (1972) found that the library skills test scores of high school students who had attended an elementary school with both a library and a librarian who conducted a strong library skills program were significantly higher than those who had not had a variety of library services and facilities during their elementary school experience.

1.2.2 Presence of Library Media Specialists

Other studies examined the value and role of professional staff in a library media center. (Gaver, 1963; McMillen, 1965; Hale, 1969; Wert, 1970; McConnaha, 1972; Loertscher & Land, 1975; Didier, 1982; and Loertscher, 1987.) *The Millbrook Report* (1990) also confirmed the importance of staffing.

- In the study by Hale (1969), SAT scores improved among students receiving library service from a professional.
- Loertscher, Ho, and Bowie (1987) found that staffing was the single most important variable in an excellent elementary library media program. This study confirmed that critical staffing consisted of a full-time professional and a full-time clerical employee.
- Wert (1970) found that librarians without a Master's degree spent more time on clerical and housekeeping duties than those with more education. Teachers in high schools served by librarians with more extensive library education gave more assignments per class requiring use of the library.
- McMillen (1965) found that students in schools with good libraries and full-time librarians performed at higher levels in reading comprehension and in knowledge and use of reference materials than students in schools with minimal or no library service.
- Loertscher & Land (1975) concluded that full-time library media specialists gave a significantly greater level of services than either part-time professional library media specialists or full-time clerical staff.
- In questionnaires completed by high school students, Kelsey (1976) established that library services and materials were rated the highest criteria for effective library programs. The second most important criterion was the librarian, followed by atmosphere, time and schedule limitations, and physical facilities.
- Didier (1982) confirmed that student achievement in reading, study skills, and use of newspapers was significantly greater at the seventh grade level in schools with professional library media personnel as compared to schools without them; and that student access to the library media center was significantly greater in schools with professional library media personnel than in schools without them.

1.2.3 Experimental Studies

A group of studies dealt with a "special treatment period" for students involving the library and measured their performance before and after that treatment.

- Bailey (1970) studied a group of disadvantaged first-grade students who participated in a library resource program over a 12-week period. The experimental group showed a significant increase in total language ability and the ability to express ideas over the control group of disadvantaged students who received no special treatment.
- DeBlauw (1973) examined the rate of cognitive growth of students on achievement test batteries before and after implementation of a multimedia program. Elementary students showed significant gains, but the academic performance of high school students was unchanged by the program.
- A longer term study of twelfth grade English students by Gilliland (1986) found that test scores on the study-locational portion of the California Assessment Program improved during the years following implementation of a library review program.
- Harmer (1959) examined the effect of library training on the summer loss or

gain in reading abilities among fourth graders in Minnesota. The experimental group in the study showed some superiority in reading retention.

- Gengler (1965) looked at differences in the ability to apply selected problem solving skills between sixth grade students who were instructed by a classroom teacher and those who received additional instruction from an elementary school librarian. Findings showed that the mean score on a problem solving skills examination for the librarian/teacher instructed group was significantly higher than for the teacher instructed group.

- Hastings and Tanner (1963) looked at whether improved English language skills could be developed at the tenth-grade level through systematic library experiences rather than the traditional emphasis on formal English grammar. The group that eliminated all traditional emphasis on formal grammar and spelling and instead received systematic work in the use of library references was significantly superior to the groups which emphasized traditional work in grammar and spelling.

- In the study by Hutchinson (1982), tenth-grade students were given special library skills instruction and practice by English teachers over a two-week period. Library usage among the students increased regardless of their academic grade point average.

- Schon (1984) and Schon, Hopkins, Everett, and Hopkins (1984-85) studied the effect of a special six-week library motivational program among elementary and junior high school students in two studies. Again, library use increased and library attitudes improved among students exposed to the special treatment.

- Eisenberg (1988) reported on a study by M. Elspeth Goodin involving high school seniors in college preparatory English classes who received a series of lessons on the research process and completed a research paper. Students in the experimental group scored significantly higher on the posttest of basic college library information than students in the control group. Students in the experimental group also produced research papers more acceptable at the college freshman level and expressed more positive attitudes toward using the college library than students in the control group.

1.2.4 Service Levels & Collection Size

A number of studies focused on service levels and collection size in relation to student achievement.

- Greve (1974) discovered that the most valuable predictor of student test scores was the number of volumes in the school library.

- Loertscher, Ho, and Bowie (1987) also emphasized the importance of collection size in the libraries of exemplary elementary schools.

- Thorne (1967) examined the reading comprehension and library skills of students using the augmented services of a Knapp Project library versus the nominal services of a second junior high school library in a two-year study. Findings revealed a significant difference in the mean gains of the experimental group over the control group in reading comprehension and library skills.

- On the other hand, Walker (1963) found no significant difference in the grade point averages of college students coming from communities with a

high level of library service versus students from communities with poor or no library service available.
- Harkin (1971) found no marked differences in the academic college records of students using high school libraries with high media-student ratios and those using high school libraries with low media-student ratios.
- Ducat (1960) found little evidence that the school library played a vital role in the total program of schools investigated.

1.2.5 Student and Teacher Attitudes

Studies focusing on student or teacher attitudes toward library service were conducted by Koga and Harada (1989) el Hagrasy (1961); and Hodges and Reeves (1985).
- The study by Koga and Harada (1989) is unique in that it investigates the attitudes of students in Australia, Japan, Korea, and Thailand toward school libraries. This study found that students with a keen attitude toward learning tend to use the library more often and demonstrate better academic achievement.
- El Hagrasy (1961) established that the reading habits and library backgrounds of teachers are important in the development of reading habits and library usage of their students.
- Hodges and Reeves (1985) found that audio-visual services of school library media centers strongly correlated with indicators of student attitudes and media center use.

1.2.6 Student's Self-Concept & Librarian's Job Satisfaction

Self-concept of students was a factor in studies by Hopkins (1989), Hale (1970), Aaron (1975), and Eisenberg (1988); while Fortin (1970) measured job satisfaction of school librarians.
- Hale (1970) found that an experimental group of twelfth grade students who were given a variety of library services and resources and the opportunity to work independently under the supervision of the librarian showed "remarkable enthusiasm" for learning.
- Aaron (1975) studied a group of eighth grade students who participated in a program in which a full-time media specialist was added to the teaching team. In addition to showing significant improvement in language arts, spelling, and math computation, the students in the experimental group experienced improvement in their self-concept.
- Eisenberg (1988) reporting research done by M. Elspeth Goodin stated that students in an experimental group that received a series of lessons on the research process were consistently more positive in their feelings of confidence in using the college library than students who received no library instruction.
- Hopkins (1989) found that library media centers can play a positive role in developing positive self-concepts in children.
- Fortin (1970) confirmed that the impact of the library on the educational program was strongly related to the work satisfaction level of the librarian.

1.2.7 Textbooks vs. Library Media Materials

Barrilleaux (1965) focused on a comparison of the achievement of junior high school students in general science classes in which textbooks were used with students who used reference materials in the school library rather than a textbook. Results showed that for all investigated educational outcomes, the use of library materials without a basic textbook was the superior method of instruction. This study, completed 25 years ago, is certainly relevant in today's instructional climate with an emphasis on resource-based learning.

1.2.8 Instructional Role of Library Media Specialists

The instructional role of library media specialists was studied by Aaron (1975), nearly 15 years prior to the publication of INFORMATION POWER.[2] Aaron found that eighth grade students who participated in an experimental program in which a full-time media specialist was added to the teaching team showed significant improvement in language arts, spelling, and math computation over the control group. Students in the experimental group also experienced improved self-confidence. Gengler (1965) also studied the impact on achievement of students receiving instruction from a classroom teacher and an elementary school librarian, and found that the mean scores for the librarian-teacher instructed group on a problem-solving skills examination was significantly higher than for those in the group instructed by the teacher alone.

---

[2]INFORMATION POWER: Guidelines for School Library Media Programs (Chicago and London: American Library Association, and Washington, D.C.: Association for Educational Communications and Technology, 1988).

THE IMPACT OF SCHOOL LIBRARY MEDIA CENTERS ON ACADEMIC ACHIEVEMENT

A TIMELINE OF THE RESEARCH

1950s

Harmer, W. R. (1959). The effect of a library training program on summer loss or gain in reading abilities. Doctoral dissertation, University of Minnesota. (University Microfilms No. 60-968)

1960s

Ducat, M. P. C. (1960) Student and faculty use of the library in three secondary schools. Doctoral dissertation. Columbia University, New York City. (University Microfilms No. 60-2449)

el-Hagrasy, S. (1961). The teacher's role in library service: an investigation and its devices. Doctoral dissertation, Rutgers University. (University Microfilms No. 61-4185)

Gaver, M. V. (1963) *Effectiveness of centralized library service in elementary schools.* (2d ed.) New Brunswick, New Jersey: Rutgers.

Hastings, D. M. & Tanner, D. (1963). The influence of library work in improving English language skills at the high school level. *Journal of Experimental Education,* 31(4), 401-405.

Walker, R. (1963). The influence of antecedent library service upon academic achievement of University of Illinois freshmen. Doctoral dissertation, University of Illinois, Champaign-Urbana, Illinois. (University Microfilms No. 64-2983)

Barrilleaux, L. E. (1965). An experimental investigation of the effects of multiple library sources as compared to the use of a basic textbook on student achievement and learning activity in junior high school science. Doctoral dissertation, University of Iowa, Iowa City, Iowa. (University Microfilms No. 66-03406)

Gengler, C. R. (1965). A study of selected problem-solving skills comparing teacher-instructed students with library/teacher-instructed students. Doctoral dissertation, University of Oregon, Eugene, Oregon. (University Microfilms No. 65-12,215)

McMillen, R. D. (1965). An analysis of library programs and a determination of the educational justification of these programs in selected elementary schools of Ohio. Doctoral dissertation, Western Reserve University, Cincinnati, Ohio. (University Microfilms No. 66-08017)

Wilson, E. J. (1965). Evaluating urban centralized elementary school libraries. Doctoral dissertation, Wayne State University, Detroit, Michigan. (University Microfilms No. 66-10123)

Thorne, L. M. (1967). The influence of the Knapp School Libraries Project on the reading comprehension and on the knowledge of library skills of the pupils at the Farrar Junior High School, Provo, Utah. Doctoral dissertation, Brigham Young University, Provo, Utah. (University Microfilms No. 67-17,224)

Yarling, J. R. (1968). Children's understandings and use of selected library-related skills in two elementary schools, one with and one without a centralized library. Doctoral dissertation, Ball State University, Muncie, Indiana. (University Microfilms No. 69-4202)

Ainsworth, L. (1969). An objective measure of the impact of a library learning center. *School Libraries,* 18 (Winter), 33-35.

Hale, I. W. (1969). The influence of library services upon the academic achievement of twelfth-grade students at Crestwood Senior High School, Chesapeake, Virginia. Athens, Georgia: Georgia University, Department of Library Education. (ERIC Document Reproduction Service No. ED 047 694)

1970s

Bailey, G. M. (1970). The use of a library resource program for the improvement of language abilities of disadvantaged first grade pupils of an urban community. Doctoral dissertation, Boston College. (University Microfilms No. 70–3369)

Becker, D. E. (1970). Social studies achievement of pupils in schools with libraries and schools without libraries. Doctoral dissertation, University of Pennsylvania, Philadelphia. (University Microfilms No. 70–22868)

Fortin, C. C. (1970). The relation of certain personal and environmental characteristics of school librarians to their life values and work satisfactions. Doctoral dissertation, University of Minnesota. (University Microfilms No. 82–14981)

Wert, L. M. (1970). Library education and high school library services. Doctoral dissertation, University of Illinois, Champaign-Urbana, Illinois. (University Microfilms No. 70–21,083)

Harkin, W. D. (1971). Analysis of secondary school library media programs in relation to academic success of Ball State University students in their freshman and sophomore years. Doctoral dissertation, Ball State University, Muncie, Indiana. (University Microfilms No. 72–07508)

McConnaha, V. (1972). The effect of an elementary school library at high school level. *California School Libraries*, 43 (Summer), 24–29.

DeBlauw, R. A. (1973). Effect of multimedia program on achievement and attitudes of elementary and secondary students. Doctoral dissertation, Iowa State University, Iowa City, Iowa. (University Microfilms No. 73–25217)

Greve, C. L. (1974). The relationship of the availability of libraries to the academic achievement of Iowa high school seniors. Doctoral dissertation, Iowa State University, Iowa City, Iowa. (University Microfilms No. 73–25217)

Aaron, S. L. (1975). Personalizing instruction for the middle school learner: the instructional role of the school media specialist. Tallahassee: Florida Department of Education.

Loertscher, D. Y. & Land, P. (1975). An empirical study of media services in Indiana elementary schools. *School Library Media Quarterly*, 4 (1), 8–18.

Kelsey, A. P. (1976). A study of the criteria for the effectiveness of secondary school libraries as perceived by selected student clients. Doctoral dissertation, Miami University, Oxford, Ohio. (University Microfilms No. 77–01003)

1980s

Didier, E. K. (1982). Relationships between student achievement in reading and library media programs and personnel. Doctoral dissertation, University of Michigan. (University Microfilms No. 82–14981)

Hutchinson, L. F. (1982). The relationship between library use and academic category among tenth-grade students. *Clearing House*, 56 (1), 34–37.

Schon, I. (1984). The effects of a special school library program on elementary students' library use and attitudes. *School Library Media Quarterly*, 12N (3), 227–231.

Schon, I., Hopkins, K. D., Everett, J. & Hopkins, B. R. (1984–85). A special motivational intervention program and junior high school students' library use and attitudes. *Journal of Experimental Education*, 53 (Winter), 97–101.

Hodges, Y., Gray, J. & Reeves, W. J. (1985). High school students' attitudes toward the library media program—What makes the difference? *School Library Media Quarterly*, 94 (4), 183–90.

Loertscher, D., Ho, M. L. & Bowie, M. M. (1987). Exemplary elementary schools and their library media centers: A research report. *School Library Media Quarterly*, 15 (3), 147–153.

Eisenberg, M. B. (1988). The transferability of library research skills from high school to college. *School Library Media Quarterly,* 17 (4), 45–46.

Hopkins, D. M. (1989). Elementary school library media programs and the promotion of positive self-concepts: A report of an exploratory study. *Library Quarterly,* 59 (2), 131–147.

Koga, S. & Harada, T. (1989). Academic achievement and the school library: An international study. Paper presented at International Federation of Library Associations General Conference and Council Meeting, School Libraries Section, Paris, 1989.

**FOR INFORMATION ABOUT PURCHASING
A COPY OF THE COMPLETE REPORT, CONTACT**

**Libraries Unlimited, Inc.,
P.O. Box 3988, Englewood, CO 80155-3988.**

INDEX

Academic Governing Boards, 164
academic performance, 128
ACCESS, 81
Access, 100
accountability, 115
America Online, 112
American Association of School Administrators, 49
American Association of School Librarians, 24, 49
American Library Association's Presidential Committee on Information Literacy, 162, 166
American Libraries, 118
American 2000: An Education Strategy, 51, 120
Andersen, Hans Christian, 35
application of principles, 145
applied outcomes (products), 21
Arts in Education, 91
assessment, 116, 121, 123, 125, 127, 129, 130
Association for Educational Communications and Technologies, 24
Association of Supervision and Curriculum Development, 79
ATLIS, 112

Bainbridge, William, L., 115, 118
Baltimore Sun, 113
barriers, 55, 56, 64, 65
Bell, Ruth, 77
Bell, Terrell, 155
Berkowitz, Robert, 30
Beyond Flexible Scheduling (Dobrot and McCawley), 67
B.J. Skinner: The Man and His Ideas (Evans), 45
bibliotherapy, 35
Blevins, Terry, 88, 89
Bobcat Bulletin, The, 112
Body Lessons (4–12), 113
Bouza-Rose, Jeanne, 95
Breen, Carol, 104
Burn, Ken, 33

Capelli, Peter, 52
CARL, 80, 81
Carnegie Foundation Report, 158
Carter (Sands), Kim, 1, 7, 21. 23, 39, 40, 60, 61, 73, 86, 120, 126
Celik, Thomas, 87, 108, 110
Change, 52
change, in actions, 119, 120, 126, 128, 131
Channel One, 113
Children's Magazine Guide, 30
Chisholm, Margaret, 166
Civil War, The (Burn), 33
Clark, Christopher M., 62
Cleveland, Harlan, 156
CNN Newsroom, 113
Coatney, Sharon, 16, 64, 66, 75, 94, 95. 119, 130
Coalition for Information Literacy, 162–164, 166
collaboration, 60, 61, 111, 117, 144, 145
collaborative efforts, 62, 145; learning, 17–19, 55, 60, 141; meetings, 142; planning, 19, 21, 22, 68
collection, 75–78, 82, 86, 97, 102, 116, 117, 130
College/School Collaboration Program of the American Association for Higher Education, 111
Colorado Department of Education, report, 76
Commissions on Higher Education, 164
communication, 100
community involvement, 88–90, 93–96
computer networks, 111
concerns, 34, 42
Cone of Learning, 46, 47
cooperative planning, 76, 77, 79
coordination, 99, 145
Coralville Summer Reading Project, 109
correlation, 115, 116, 118
cultural diversity, 34–37
curriculum add-ons, 13; needs, 78; reform, 9, 10, 19, 138

Dangremond, Susan, 12, 14, 62, 64, 71, 72, 83, 106, 107, 123, 137, 138, 140, 142, 144, 146
database, 6
deterrent to change, 131
disciplinary problems, 126, 127
Dobrot, Nancy L., 18, 21, 38, 40, 44, 59, 67, 100, 124, 126, 132, 133
documentation, 119, 127
Doubts & Certainties, 63
Doyle, Christina S., 52
Drucker, Peter, 6
duplication of resources, 101

Edison, Melinda, 104
educational outcomes, 115, 129
Educator's Newsletter, 102
Edwards, Robert, 118
Eisenberg, Michael B., 23, 30
Eisenhower National Clearinghouse for Mathematics and Science Education, 78, 79
electronic mail, 112, 114
equipment, 78, 79
ESL Partners, 89
evaluation, 140, 142. *See also* assessment
Evans, R., 45

fixed library schedule, 56–59
flexible schedules, 58, 59, 144, 144
funding, 77, 81, 82, 84, 86

Geiger, Susan, 21, 122, 123, 126
global awareness, 36; culture, 61; economy, 53
Gone with the Wind (Burn), 33
GTE, 79, 105

Harada, Violet, 103, 104
Harvey, Janadene, 12, 31, 43, 66, 77, 83, 84, 122, 137
Haycock, Carol Ann and Ken, 23
Higher Education and the American Resurgence (Newman), 158
Historic Pages (4–12), 114
Hopper, William, 91
Huebler, Kitty, 48
Humphrey, Jack W., 41, 42

Illinois School Library Media Organization, 68
illiteracy, 40, 41
impatience, 56, 64
Implementing the Colorado State Board of Education Goals through School Library Media Programs, 54
inadequate resources, 56, 63
incentives, 62, 139, 140
independent learners, 63
individualized approach, 33
Information Age, 3, 5
Information: anxiety, 7; definition of, 1; detectives, 10; explosion, 4; l iterate, 3, 4, 6; management skills, 2, 5, 23; savvy, 11; skills, 21, 29; sources of, 7; specialists, 73; technology, 45, 46, 48–51
information literacy, ix,11, 23; definition of, 10; Final Report, 3, 10
information management curriculum plan, 24
Information Is Power, 138
Information Power: Guidelines for School Library Media Programs, 24, 75, 136, 138, 145
Initial Experience, 93
in-service, 65–67, 69, 70, 137
Instructor, 102
integrated approach and program, 14; curriculum, 145
integration of services, 12, 20
International Dictionary of Education, 12
Internet, 111, 112

Journey of 1000 Miles (Strachan), 36

keys, 21, 22
KIDNET, 112
Knowledge Executive, The (Cleveland), 156
Kolarik, Chris, 90
Krashan, Stephen, 42
Krasner, Lillian, 95

Lamkin, Bernice, 132, 138
Lattanzio, Marian, 100–102
learning outcomes, 21, 22
Libraries for the National Education Goals, 51
library media center, 99, 109, 131, 145; impact of, 117
Library Media Centers (LMCs), 116, 117
library media specialist, 71–76, 79, 86, 108; importance and role of, 76
lifelong habits, 113; learning, 10, 14, 17, 58, 82, 99, 107, 110, 114, 147; readers, 40, 98, 110

mainstreaming, 32
Math and Science Mentors, 89
McCawley, Rosemary, 67, 124
McClure, Robert, 121
Meyer, Herbert E., 155
mission statement, 106, 135, 136
Monster in the Third Dresser Drawer, The (Smith), 108
multimedia package, 24, 25

NASSP Bulletin, 133
National Association of Partners in Education, Inc. (NAPE), 87
National Center for Education Statistics, 42
National Center on the Educational Quality of the Workforce, 52
National Education Association, 49
National Education Association National Center for Innovation, 63
National Education Goals, 32, 50, 52, 54, 115, 120
National Forum on Information Literacy, 52, 79, 87
National School District Partnership Survey, 87
Newman, Frank, 158
Newspaper Fun with Garfield (K–3), 113
Newspapers, 113, 114
Newspapers in Education (NIE), 34, 113
New York Times, 96

outcome-based approach, 68

Pacholl, Dean, 30, 60, 72, 140
paradigm, 133, 134; shifts, 12, 14, 15
parental involvement, 119
partnering, 87, 88, 102, 104, 141, 142, 144
partnership, 101, 105–107, 110, 141–143, 146
Phi Delta Kappan, 41
pilot projects, 136, 140, 142
portfolios, 129
Power of Reading: Insights from the Research, The (Krashen), 42, 45
Prescription for Environmental Health (6–12), 114
Presidential Blue Ribbon Award, 119
principal, 132, 133, 139, 146
priorities, 69, 83, 134, 135
Prodigy, 112
products, 122, 123, 129
public access catalogs (PACs), 81, 102
Public Television, 113

Reading Helpers program, 93
Reading In and Out of School, 42, 98
Read Me a Story program, 93
Redbook, 91
reference materials, 30
research skills, 27
resistance, 56, 58, 60–62, 65
resource-based instructional unit, 16
resource-based learning, 8, 11, 36, 38, 43, 54–56, 58, 62, 64, 66–70, 132; as an approach, 13, 34, 63, 117; as a component of technology, 45, 46; benefit of, 33, 39, 40, 56, 61, 133, 134, 146; definition of, 12; goals of, 12; outcomes of, 52, 146; philosophy of, 135, 136; programs, 18; requirements of, 60; units, 24, 25, 30; vocabulary, 137, 138
resources needed, 75, 76
restructuring, 120, 121
Rhodes, Fran, 14, 19, 39, 83, 122, 130, 133, 139, 140, 145, 146
Rockin' Readers, 89
Rolton, Gloria, 35
Rules for the Administration of the Accreditation of School Districts, 67

Schiffman, Shirl, 48
SchoolMatch, 118
Science Experiments on File, 102
Seaman, Mrs. Norma, 97
Senior Pen Pals, 89
Skorupski, Diane, 64
Skrzeczynski, Chris, 84, 85
Smith, Janice Lee, 108
Snider, Susan C., 68
staff development, 65–67, 69, 139
staffing, 71–73, 76, 116, 117, 127
State Department of Education, 164
state government offerings, 68, 69
Strachan, Ian, 36
Stripling, Barbara K., 23
student outcomes assessment, 9
SUNY 2000: College Expectations: The Report of the SUNY Task Force on College Entry-Level Knowledge and Skills, 148

Taking the Lead (3–6), 113
Taproot: Journal of the New Hampshire Educational Media Association, 65
teacher/media specialist team, 144
Thompson, James C., 118, 119, 133, 134
Thormeyer, Alan, 34, 55, 62, 130
Tirone, Ellen, 65, 142

Ugly Duckling, The (Andersen), 35
U.S. Department of Education, 76
U.S. West Foundation, 50

van Deusen, Jean Donham, 24, 72, 107, 110, 123, 144
vision, 72, 134, 136, 138, 141, 142, 146
volunteers, 73, 75, 88–95
Voyage of the Mimi, The, 25

Wall Street Journal, 6
Walton, Victoria, 25
Washington Post, 34, 50
Washington Post's Educational Leadership Award, 34
Washington State's Information Skills Curriculum, 22
Watts, Betty and Craig, 93
Western Technology Dream Project, 37, 49, 50
White House Conference on Library and Information Services, 166
Whittle Communications, 112
whole language, 44, 45
Wilder, Laura Ingalls, 124
World of Uniqueness, A, (5–8), 114
Wurman, Richard Saul, 7

Youth News Service (YNS), 114

Zobec, Helena, 100